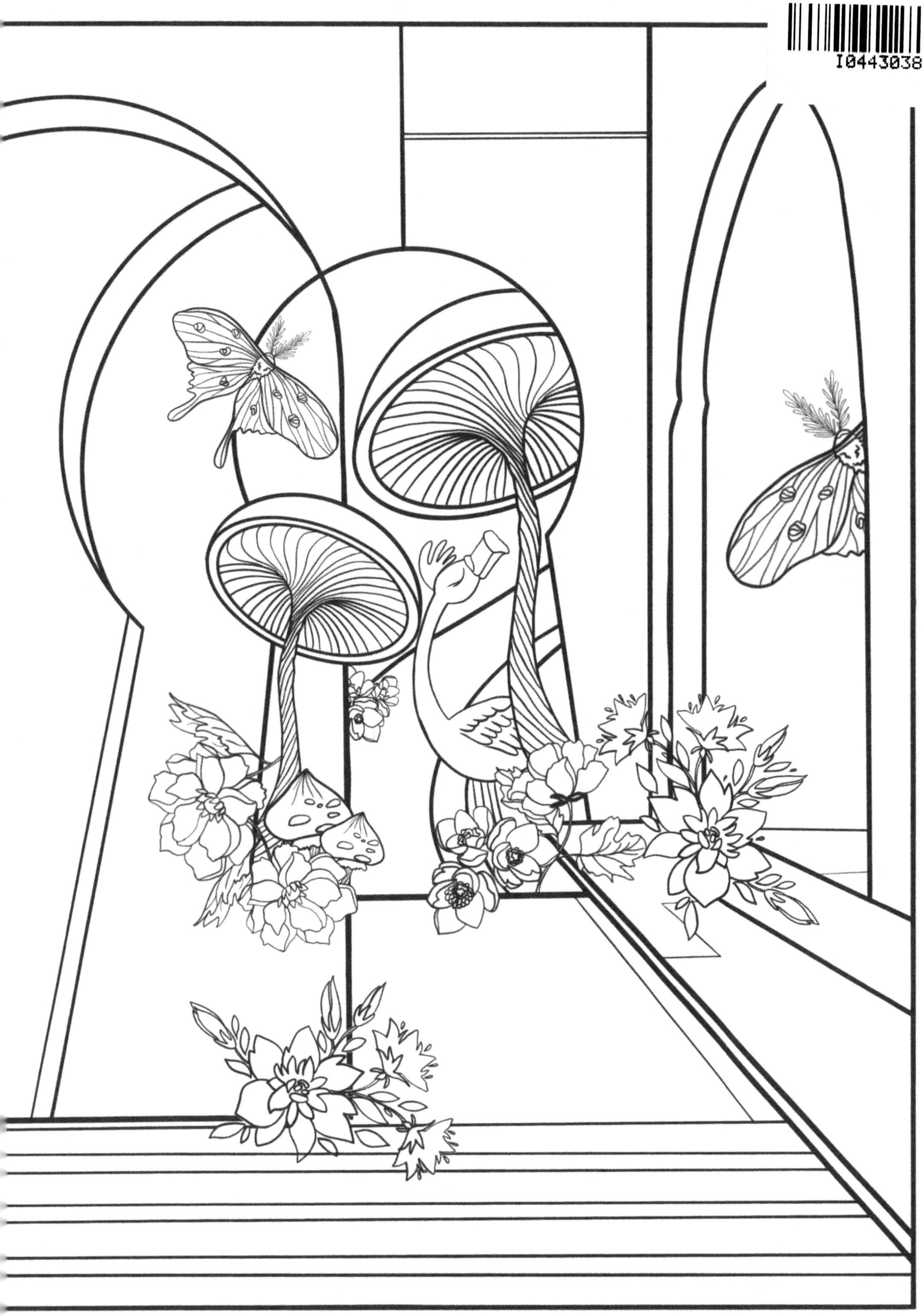

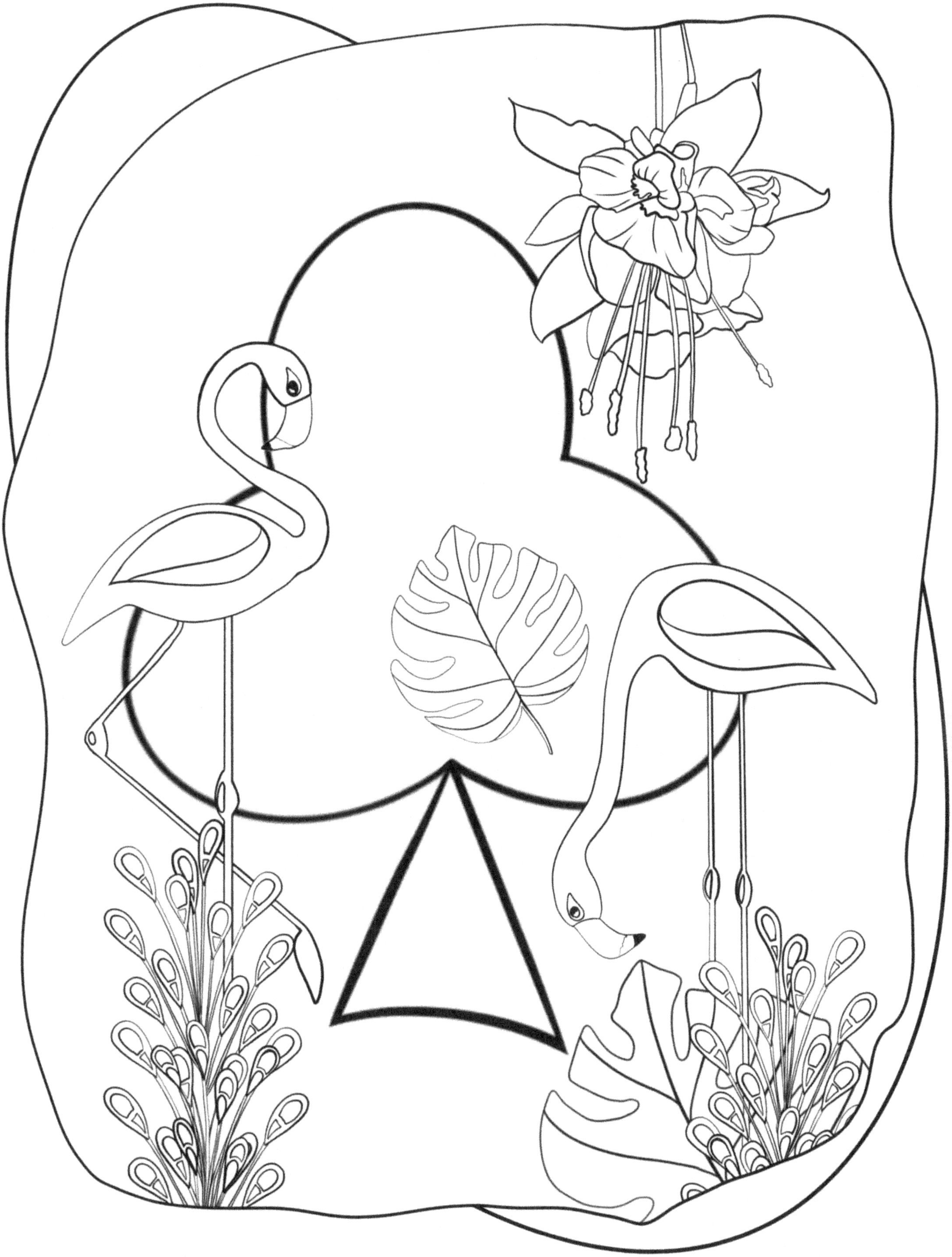

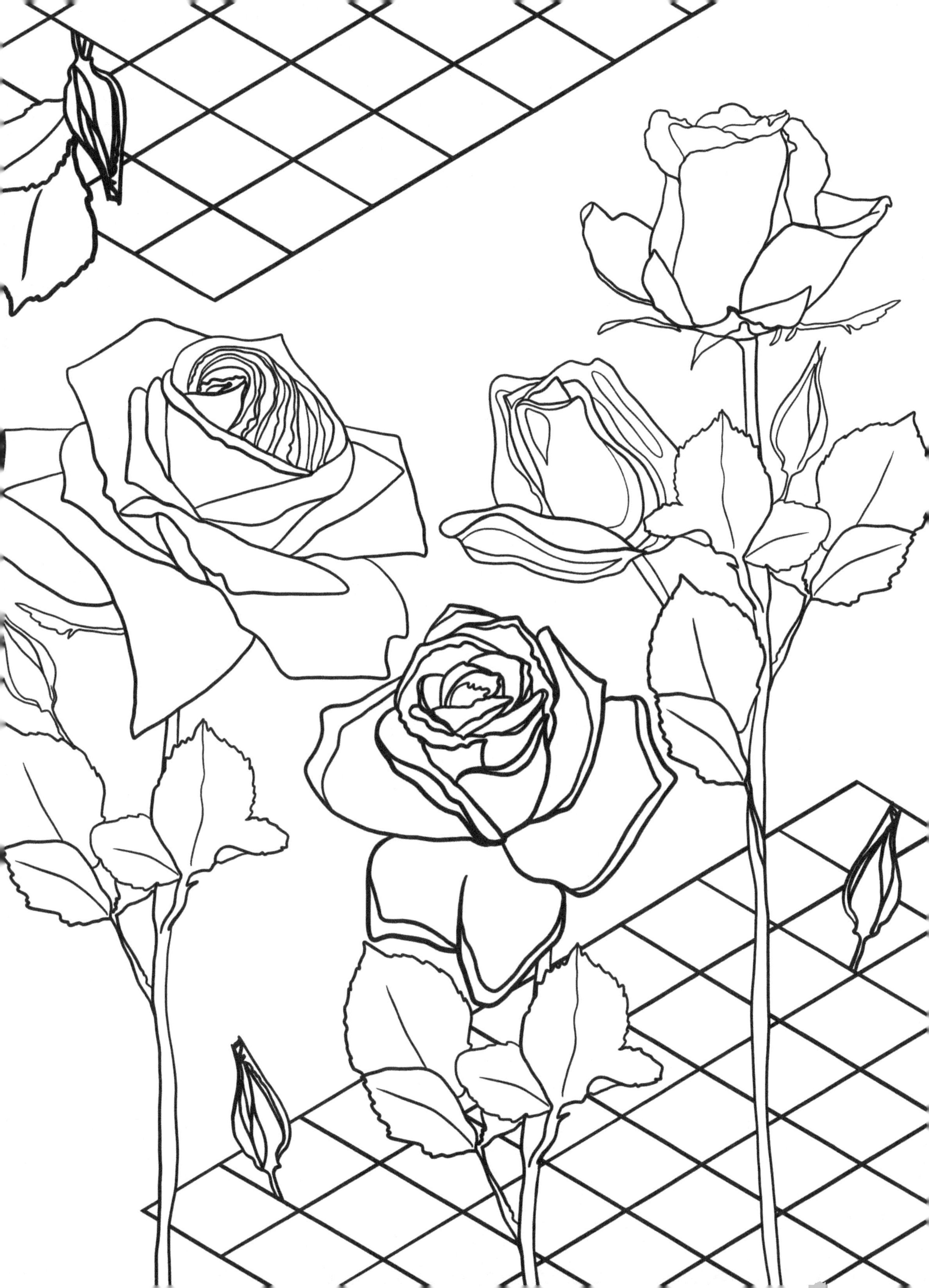

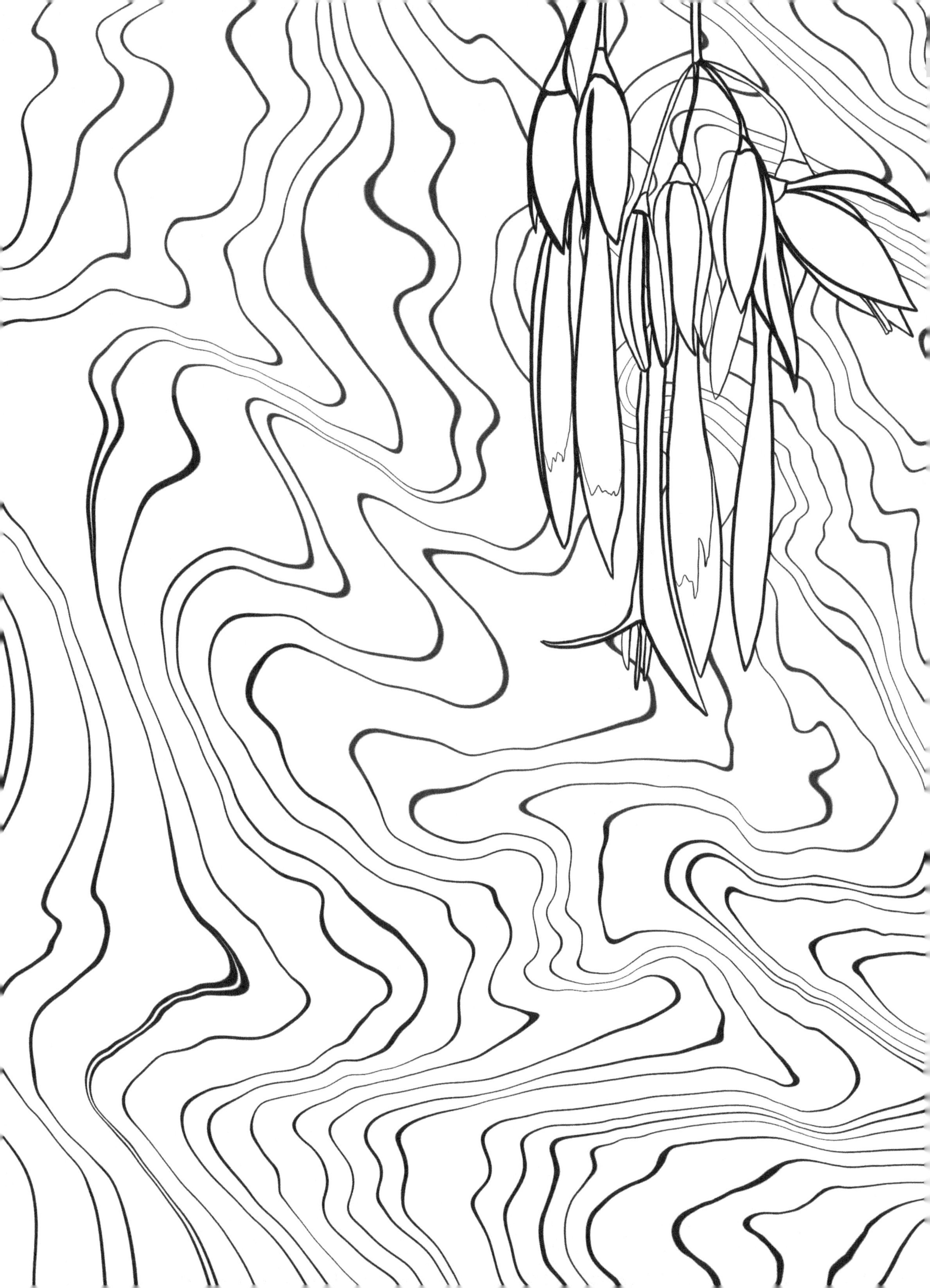

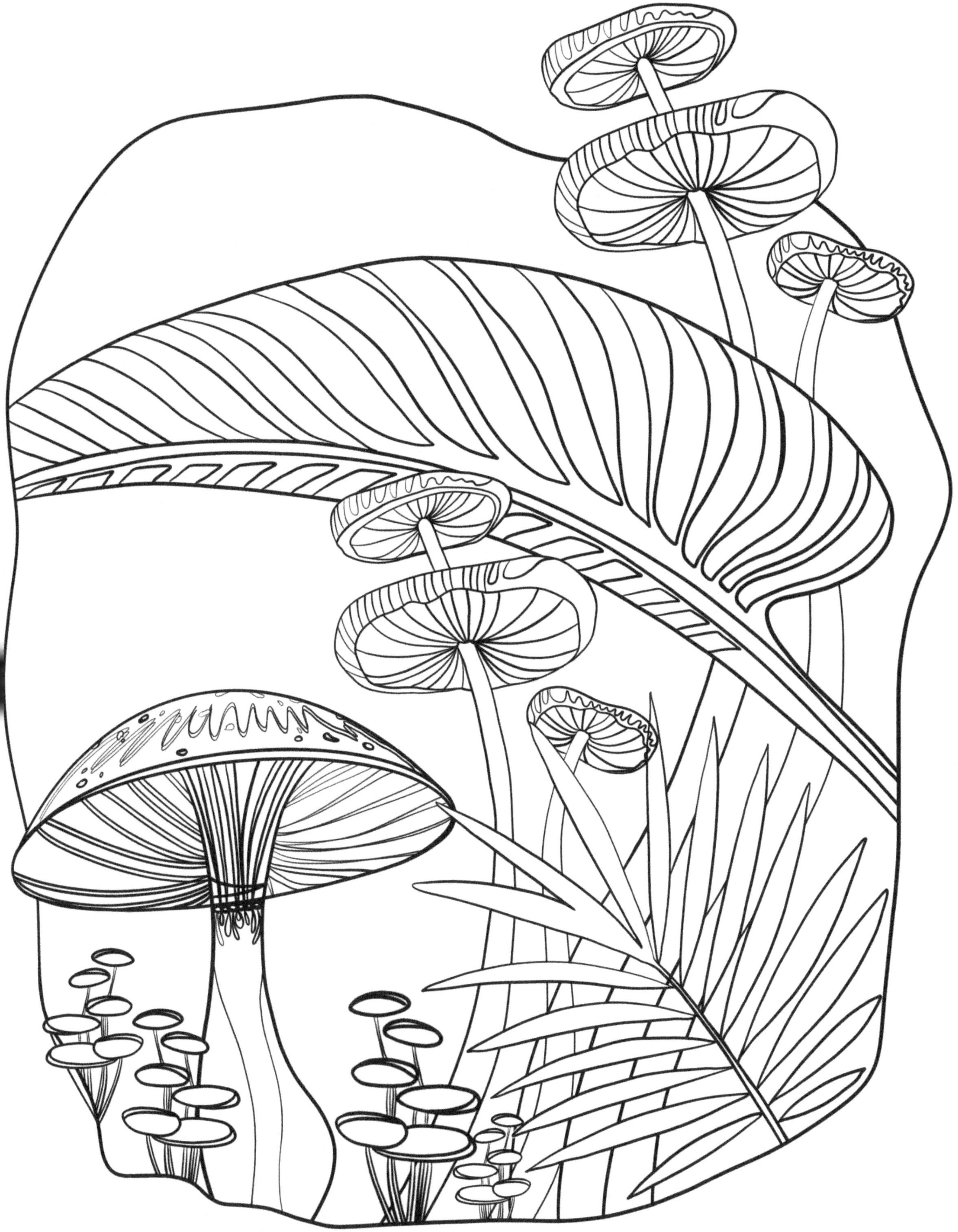

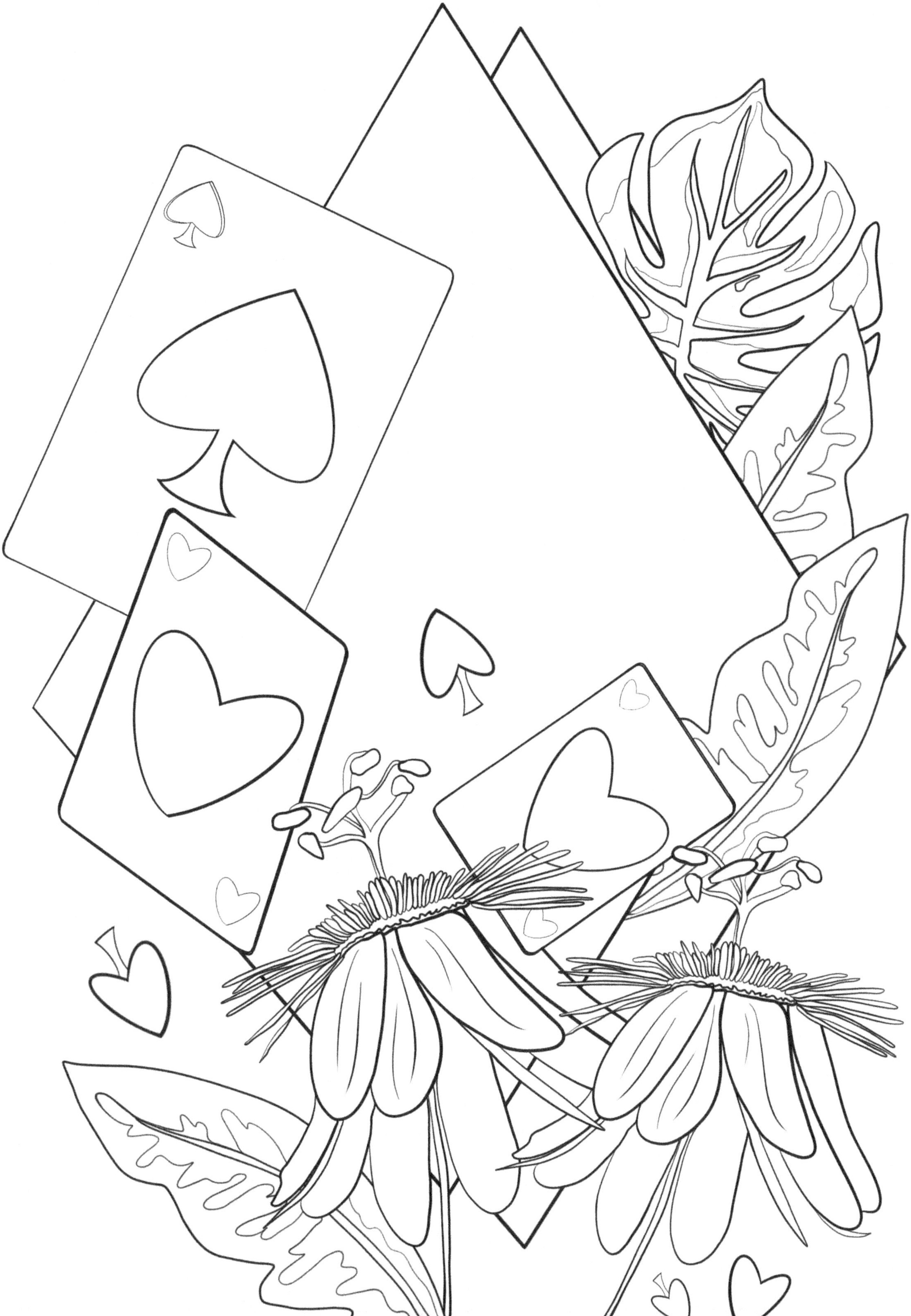

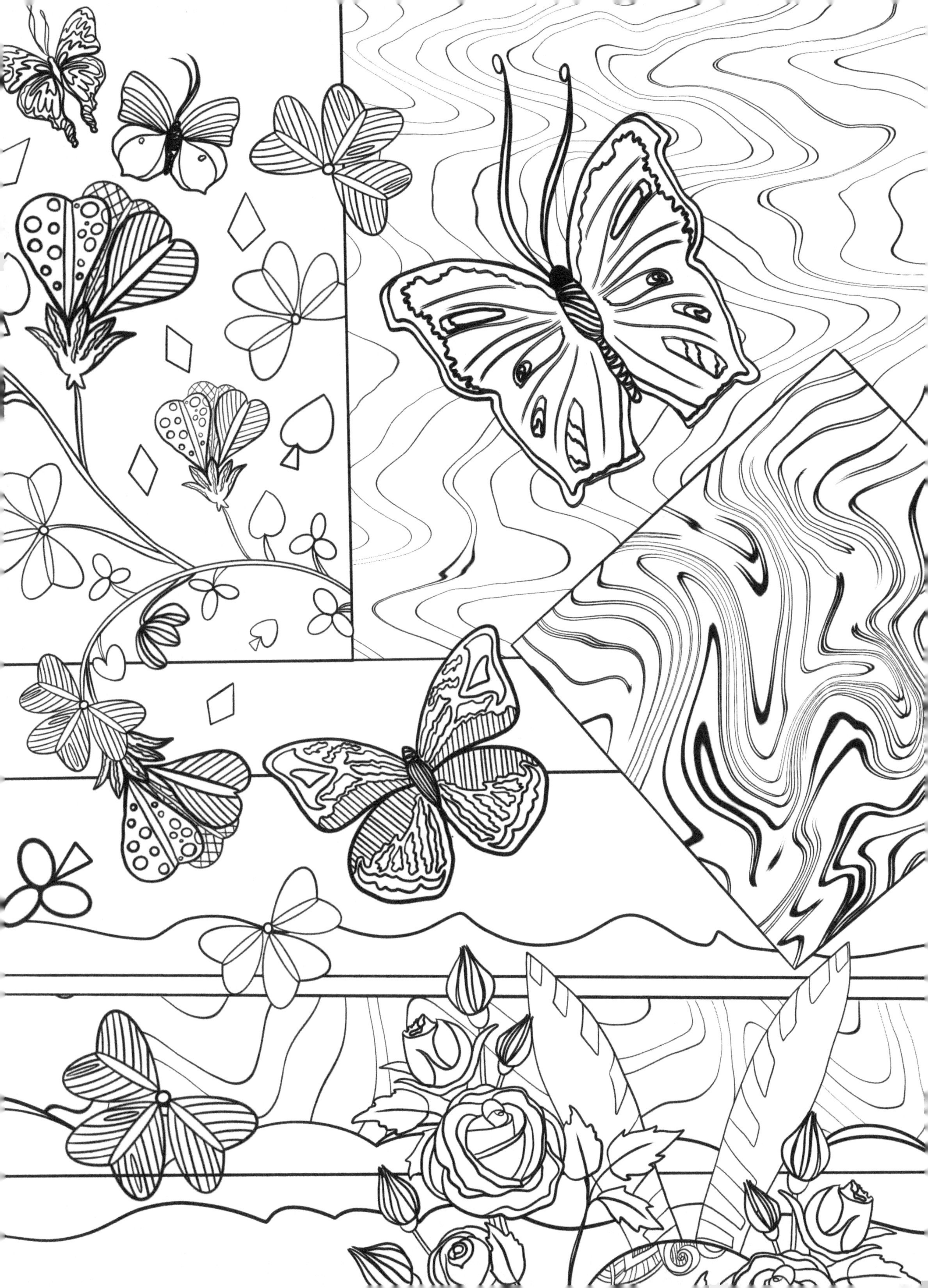

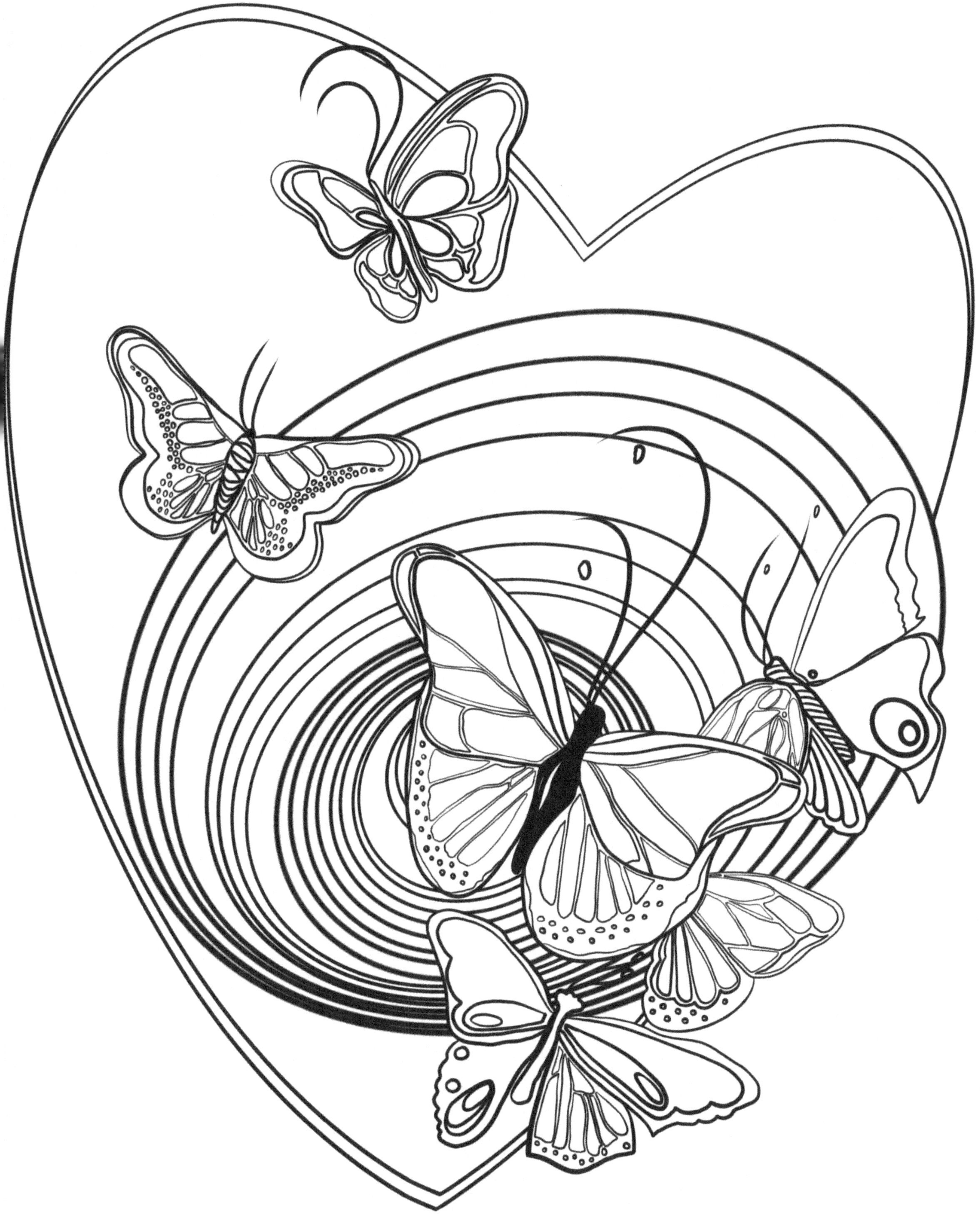

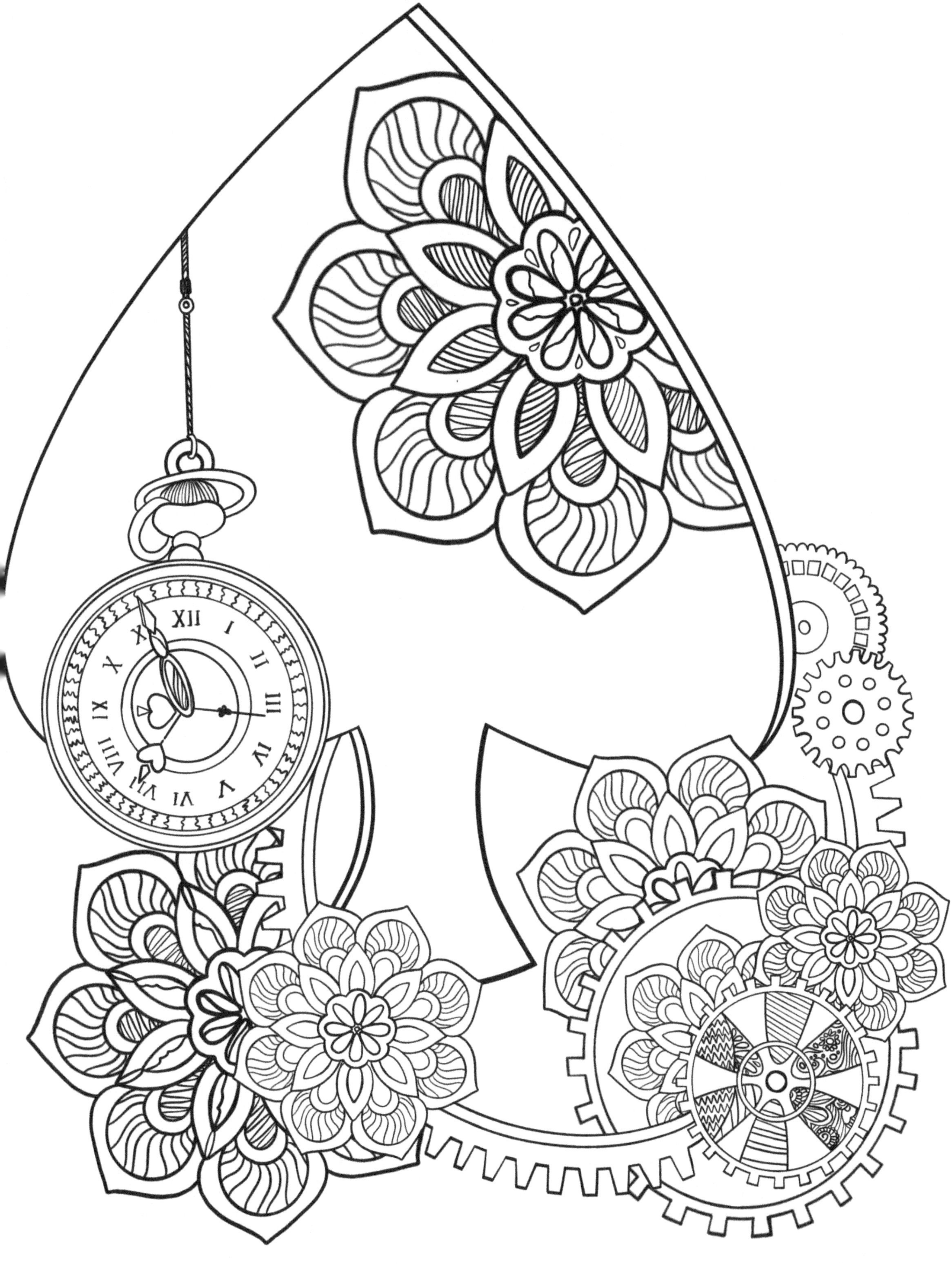

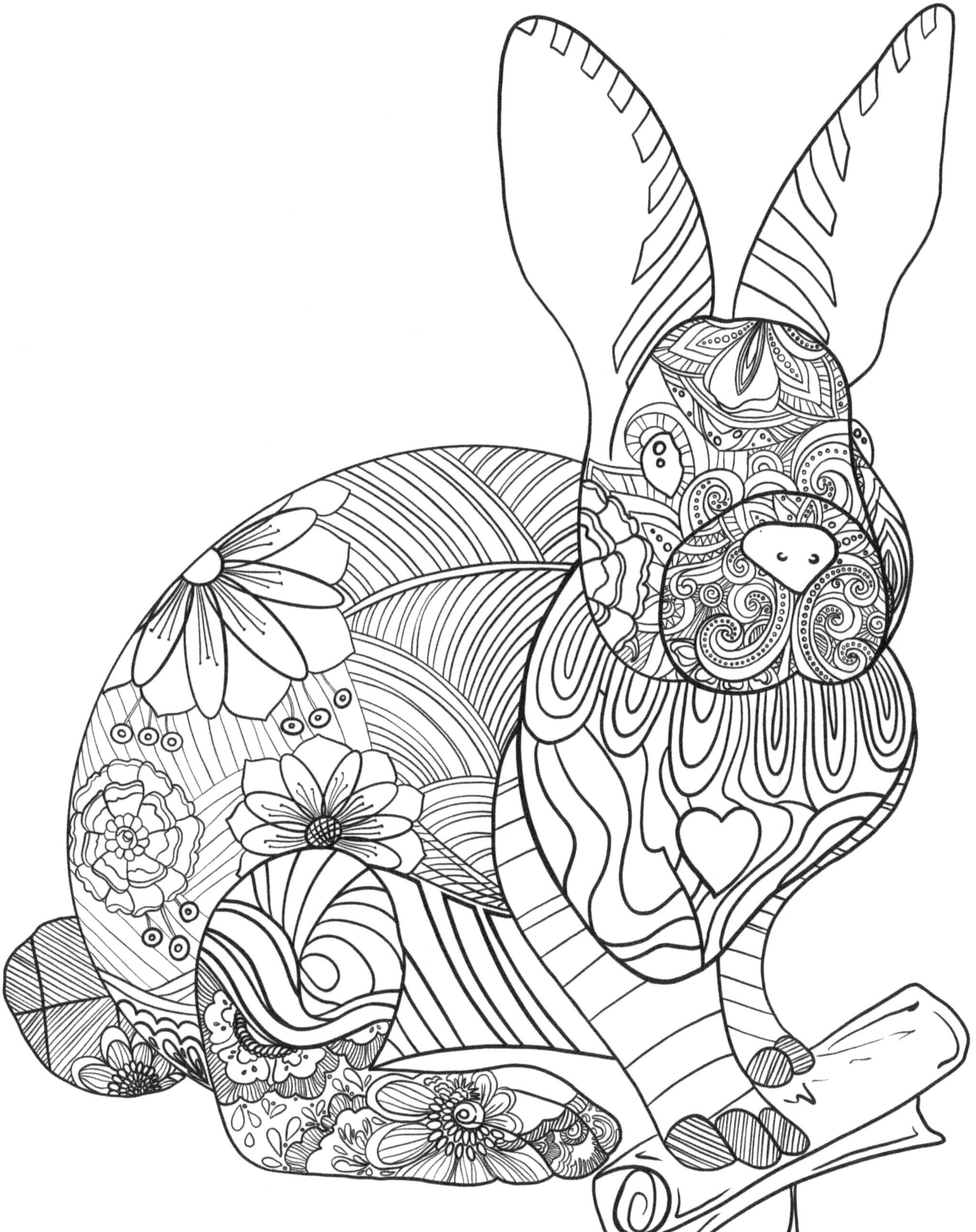

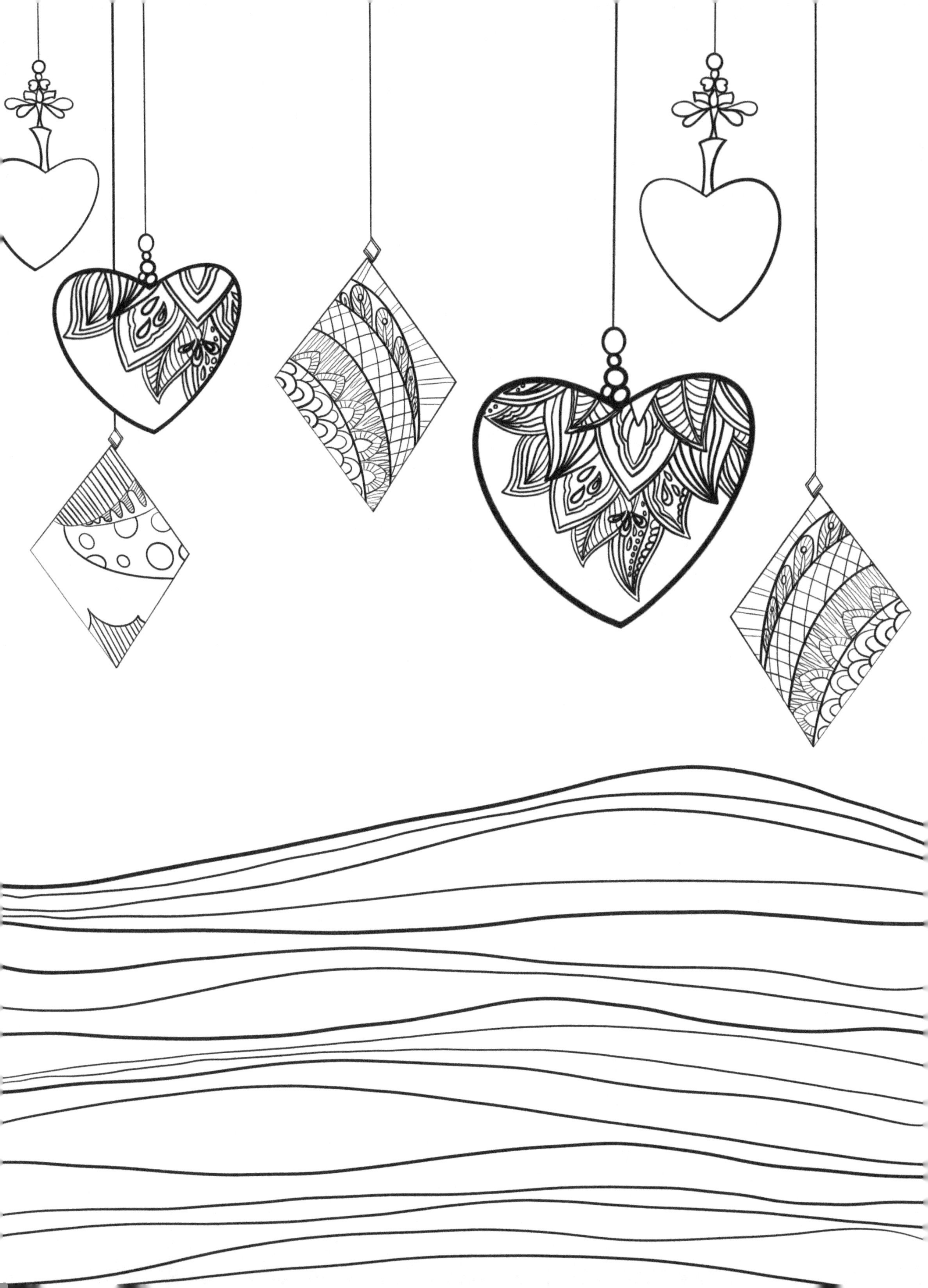

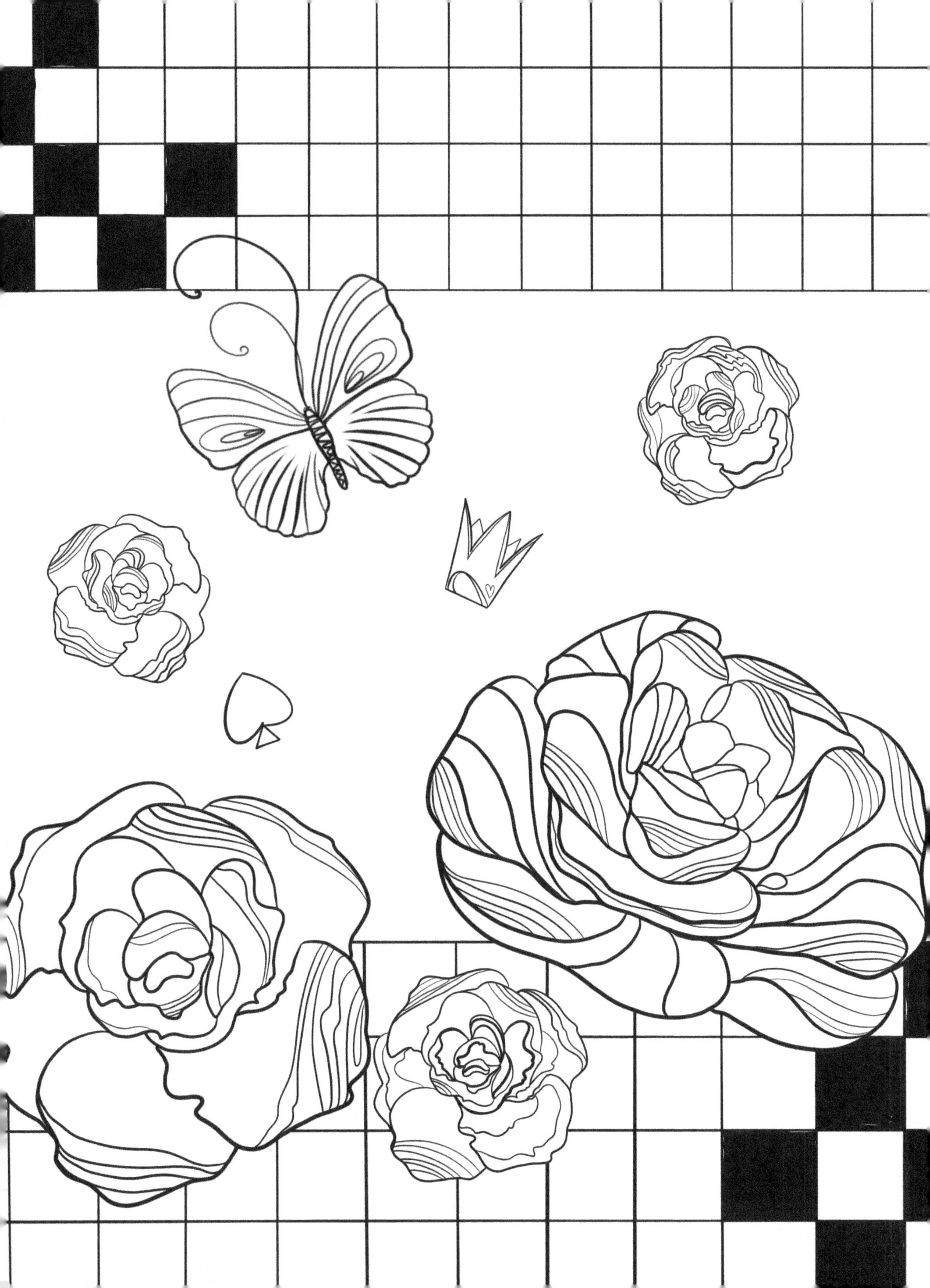

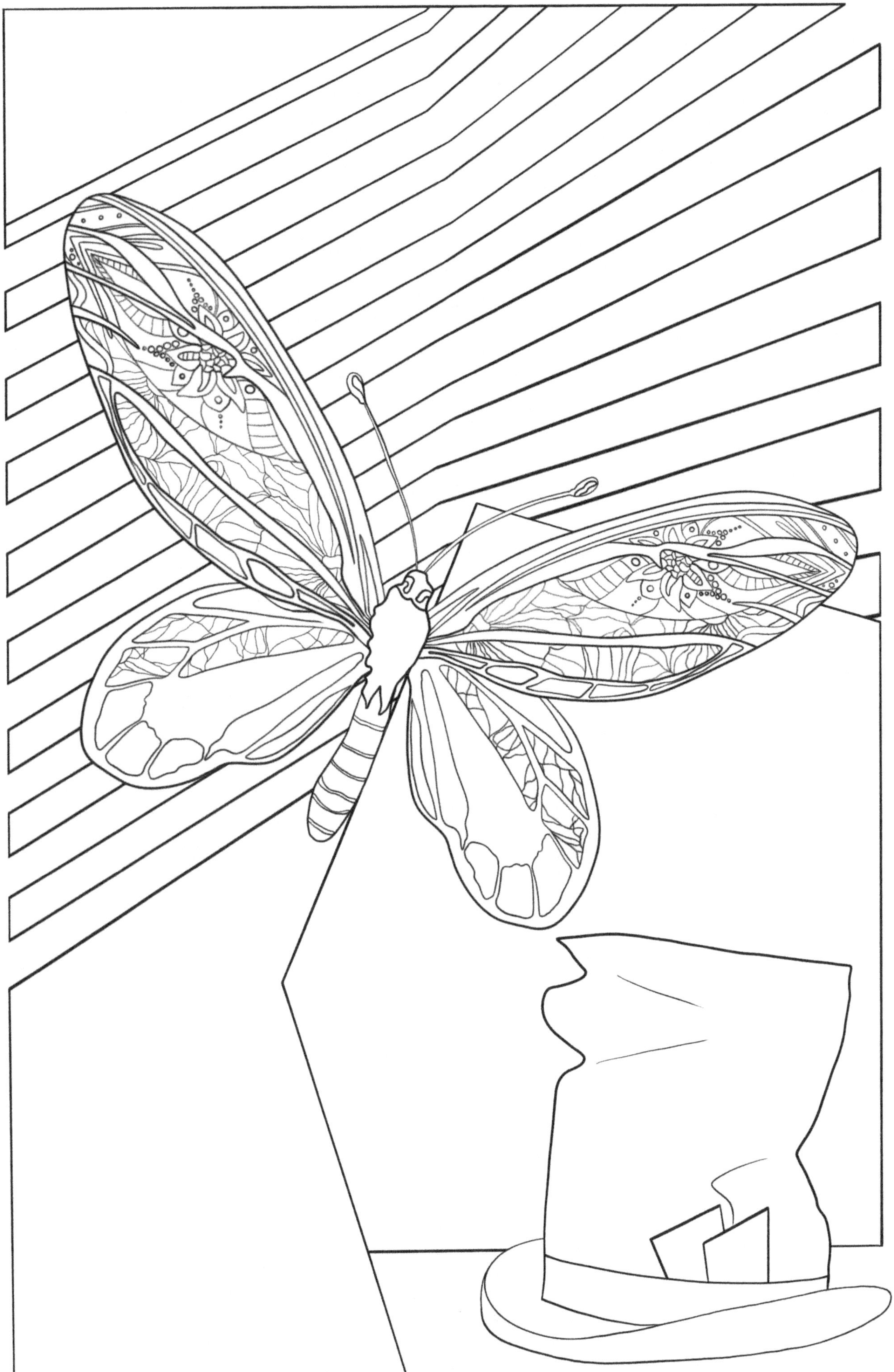

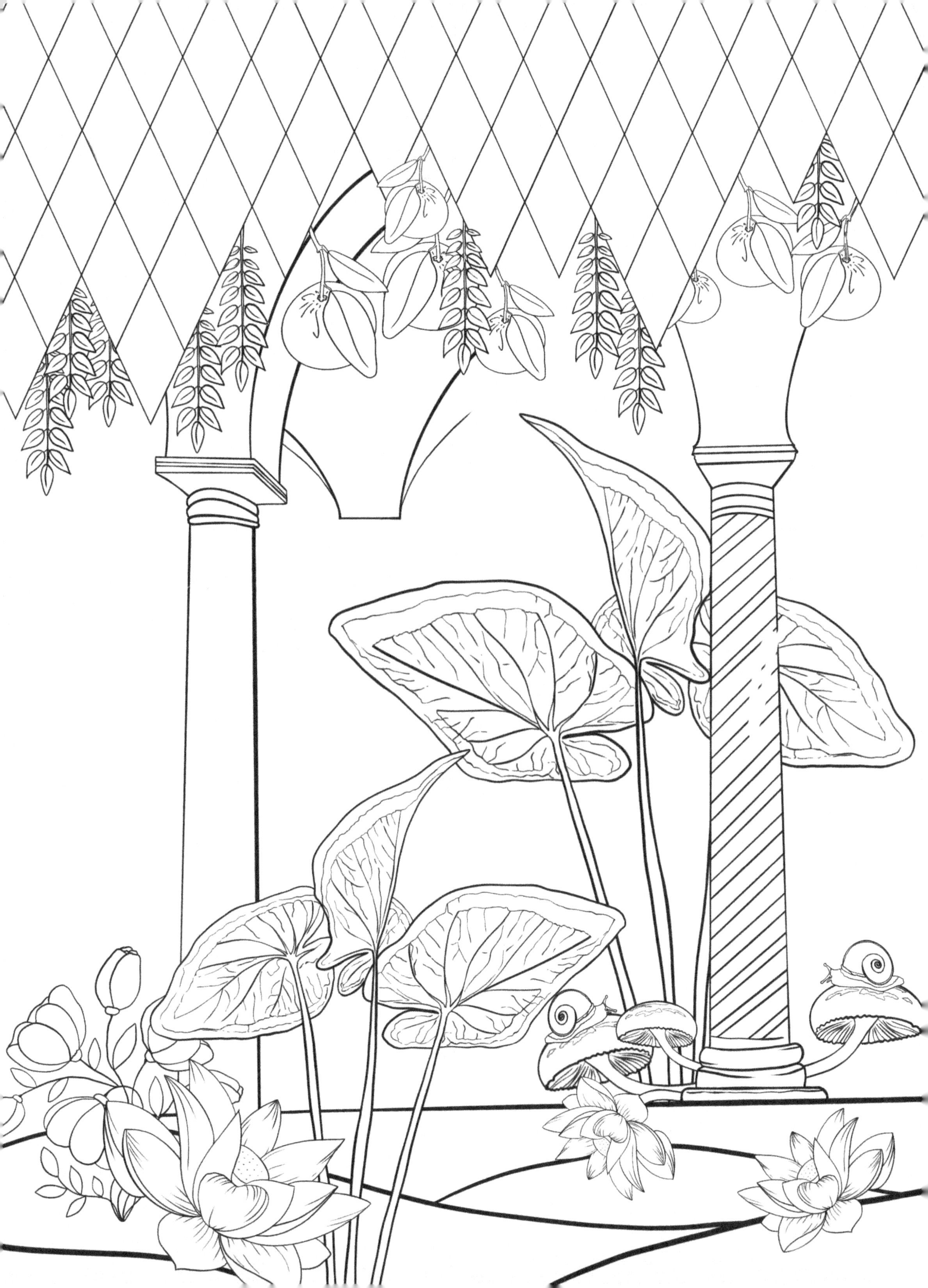

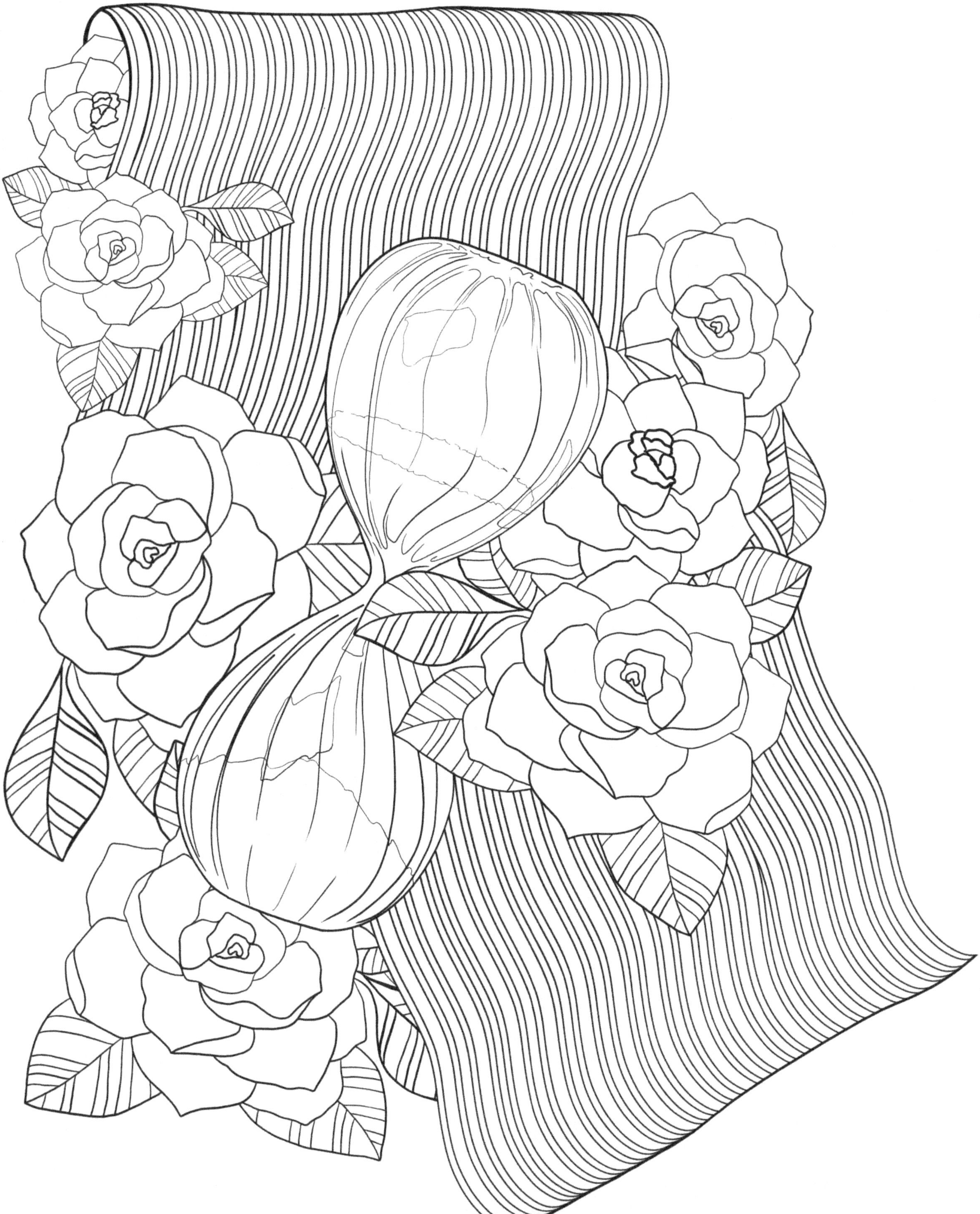

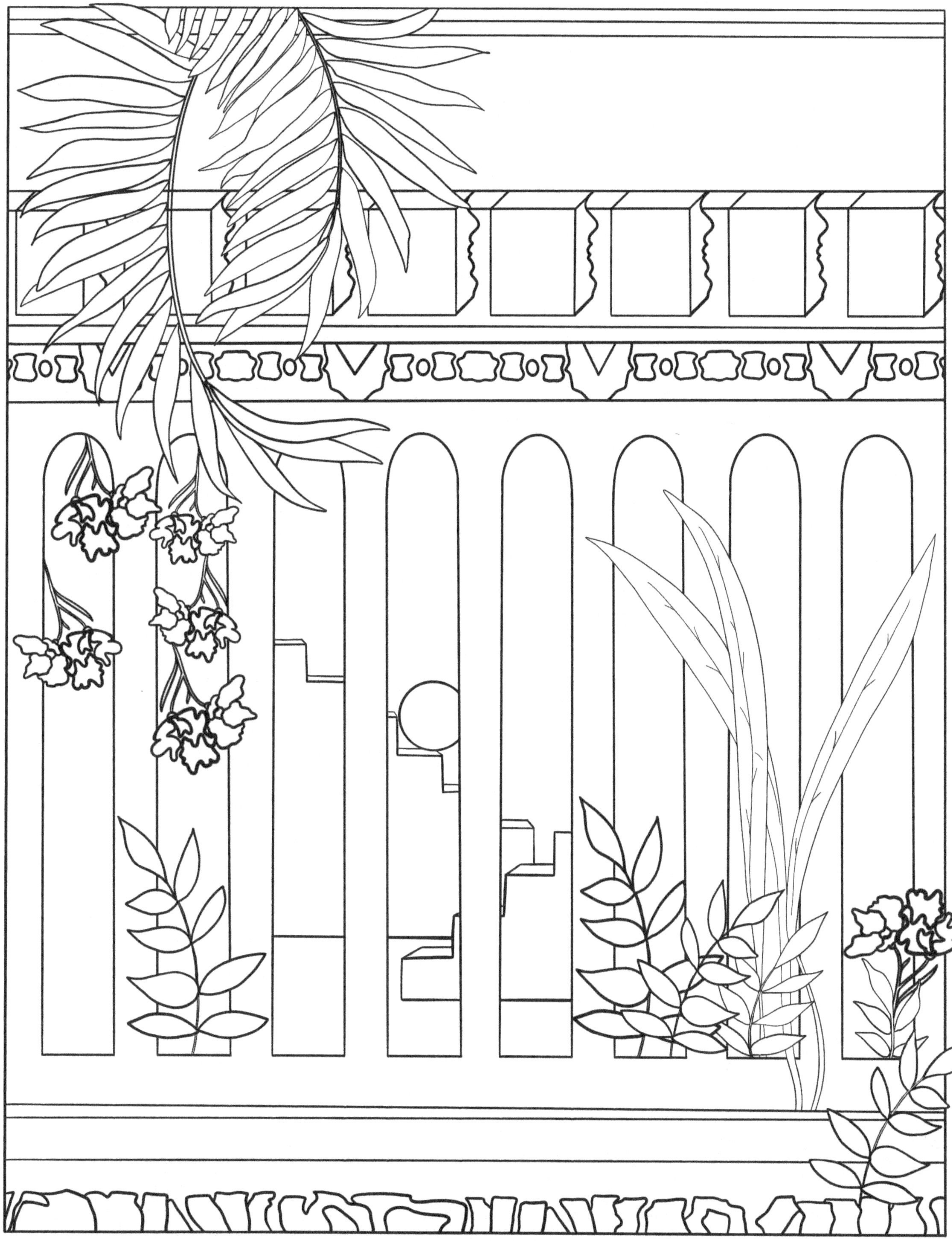

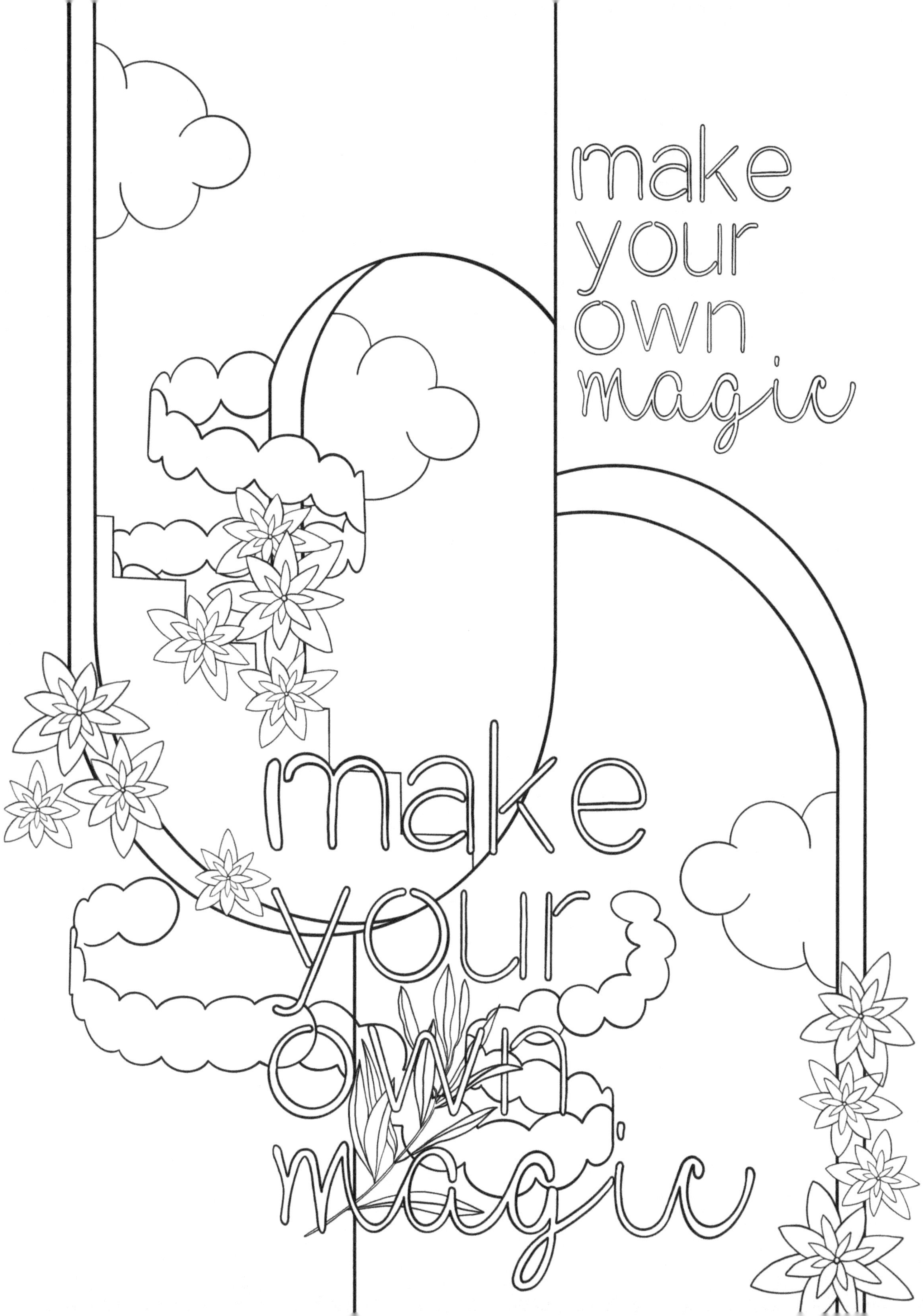
make
your
own
magic
make
your
own
magic

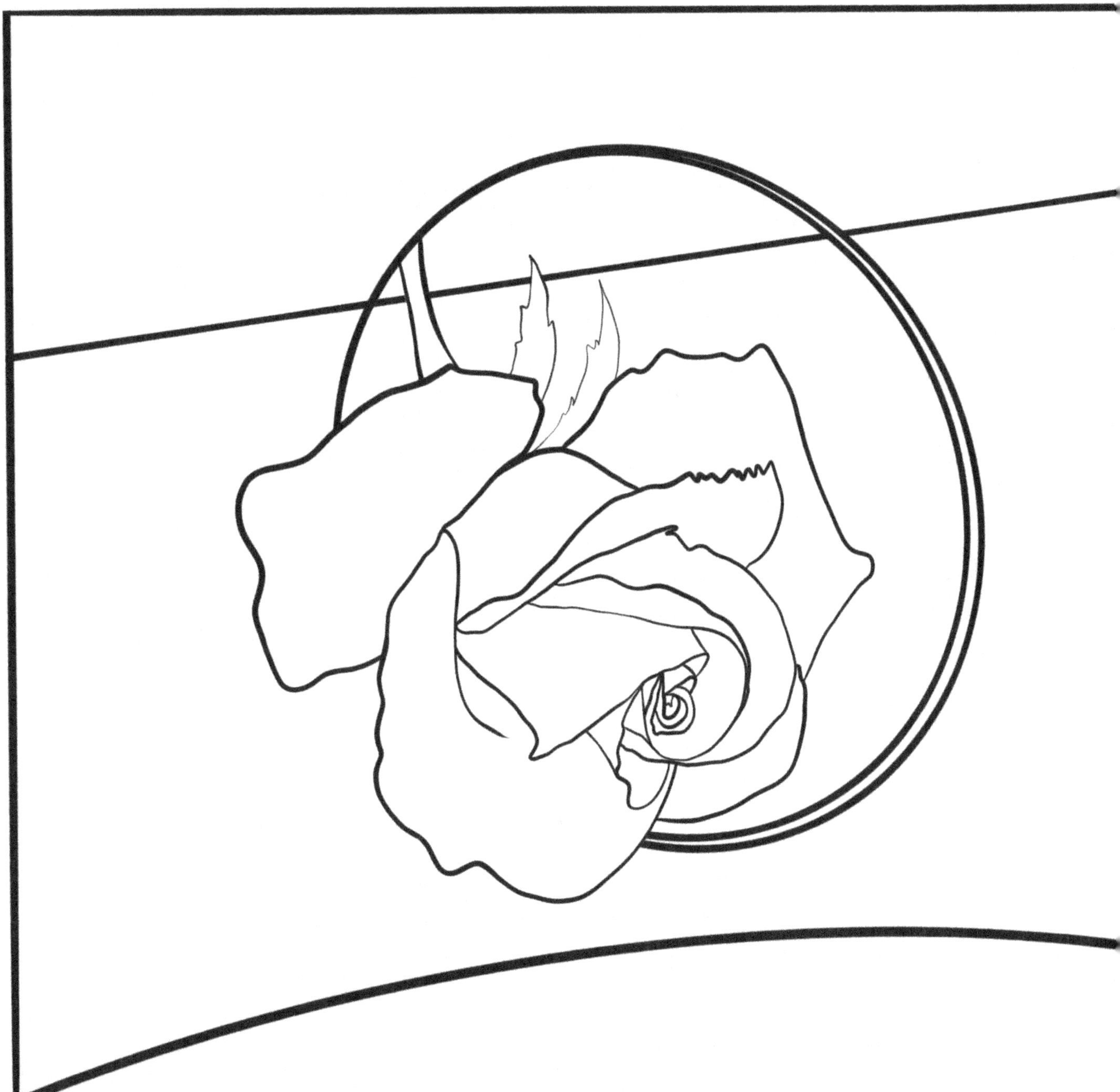

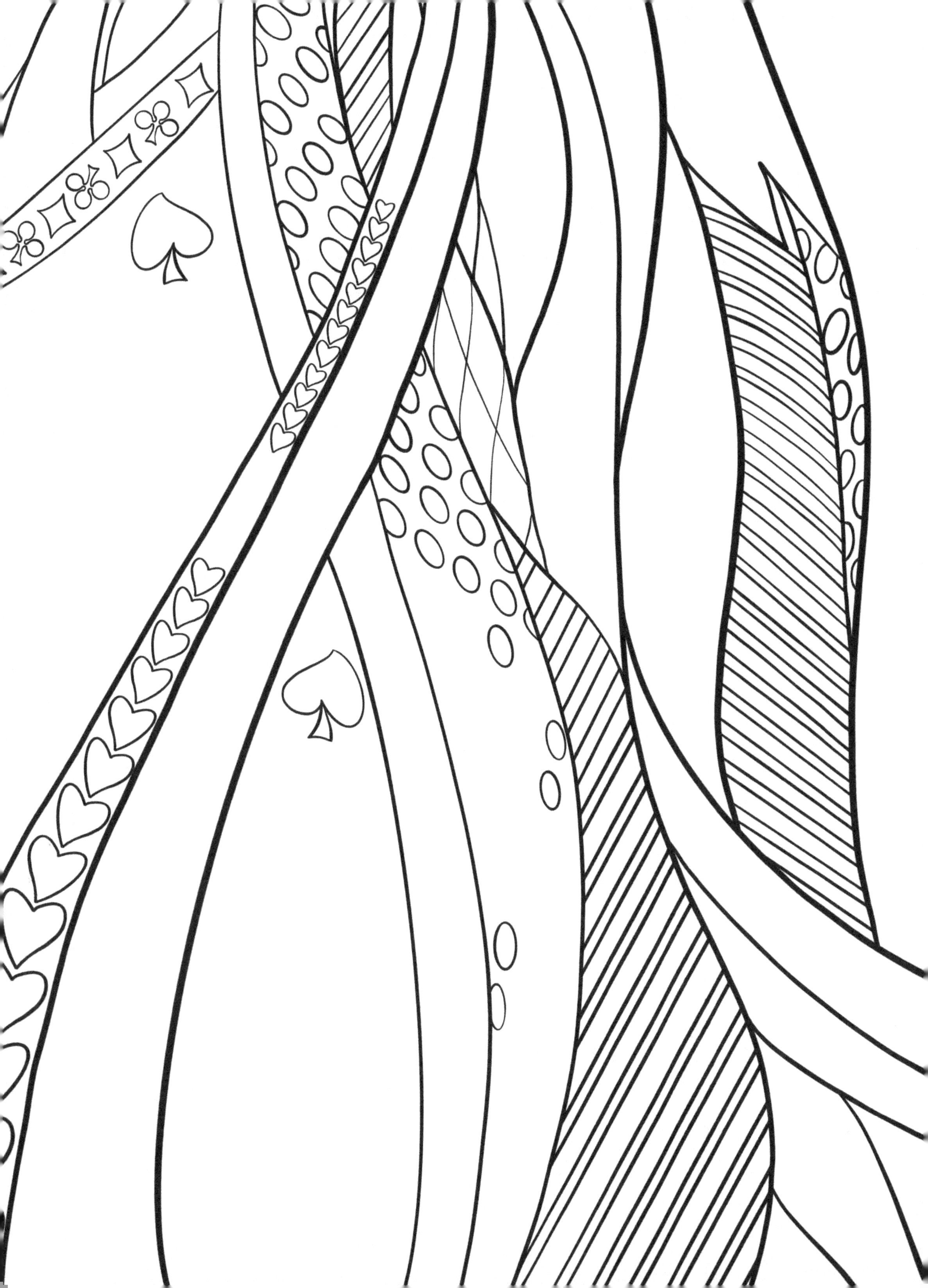

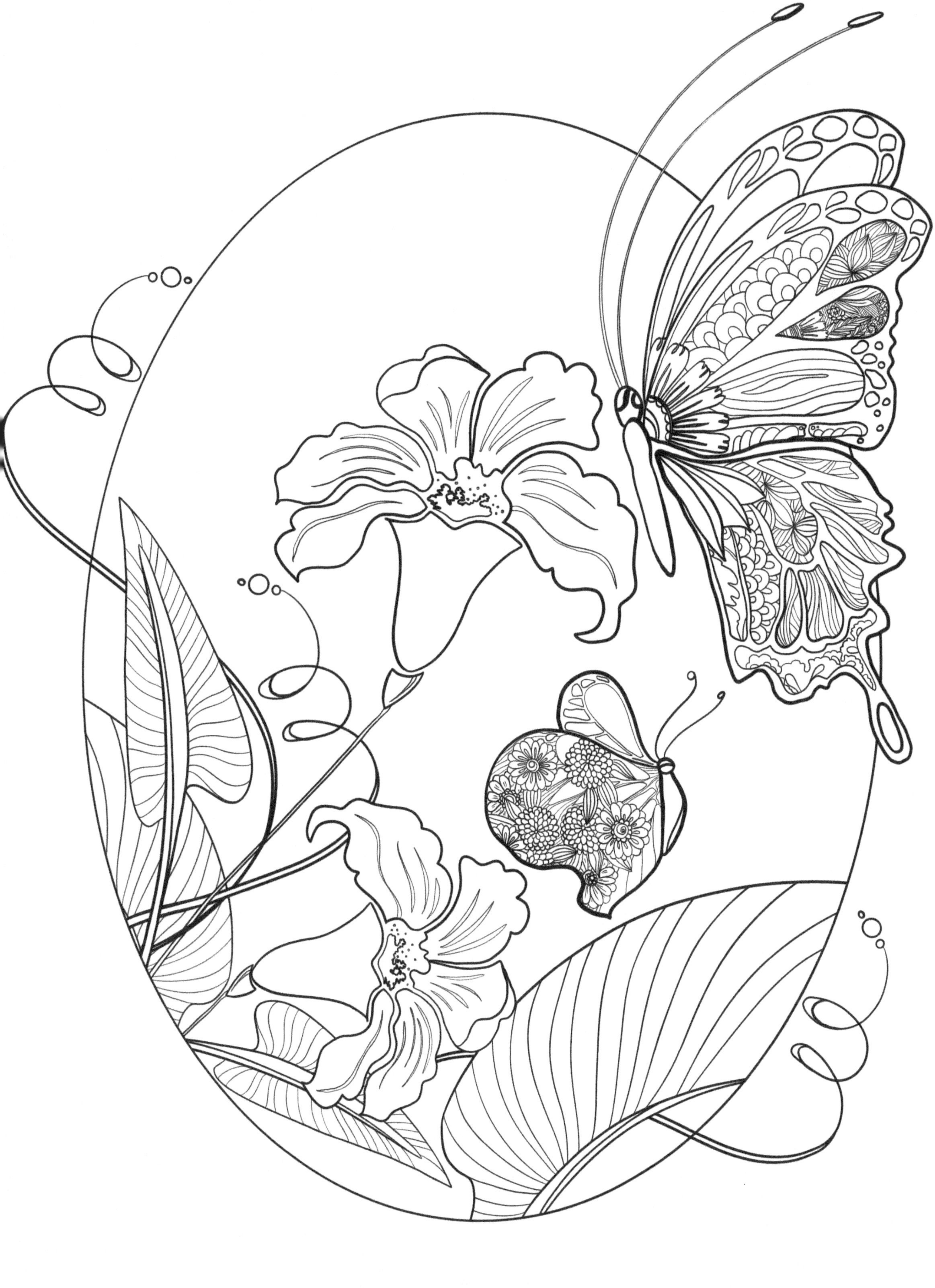

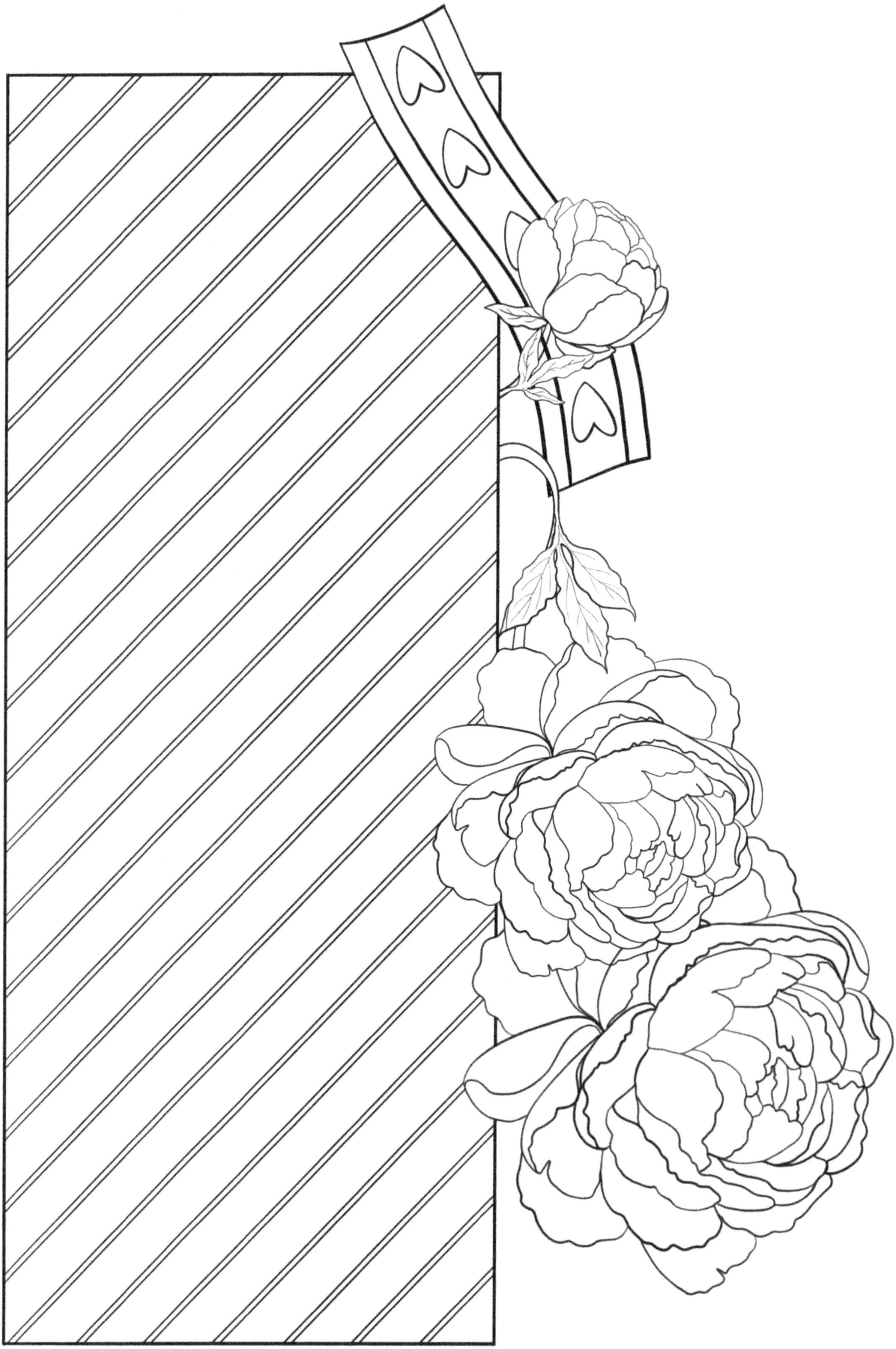

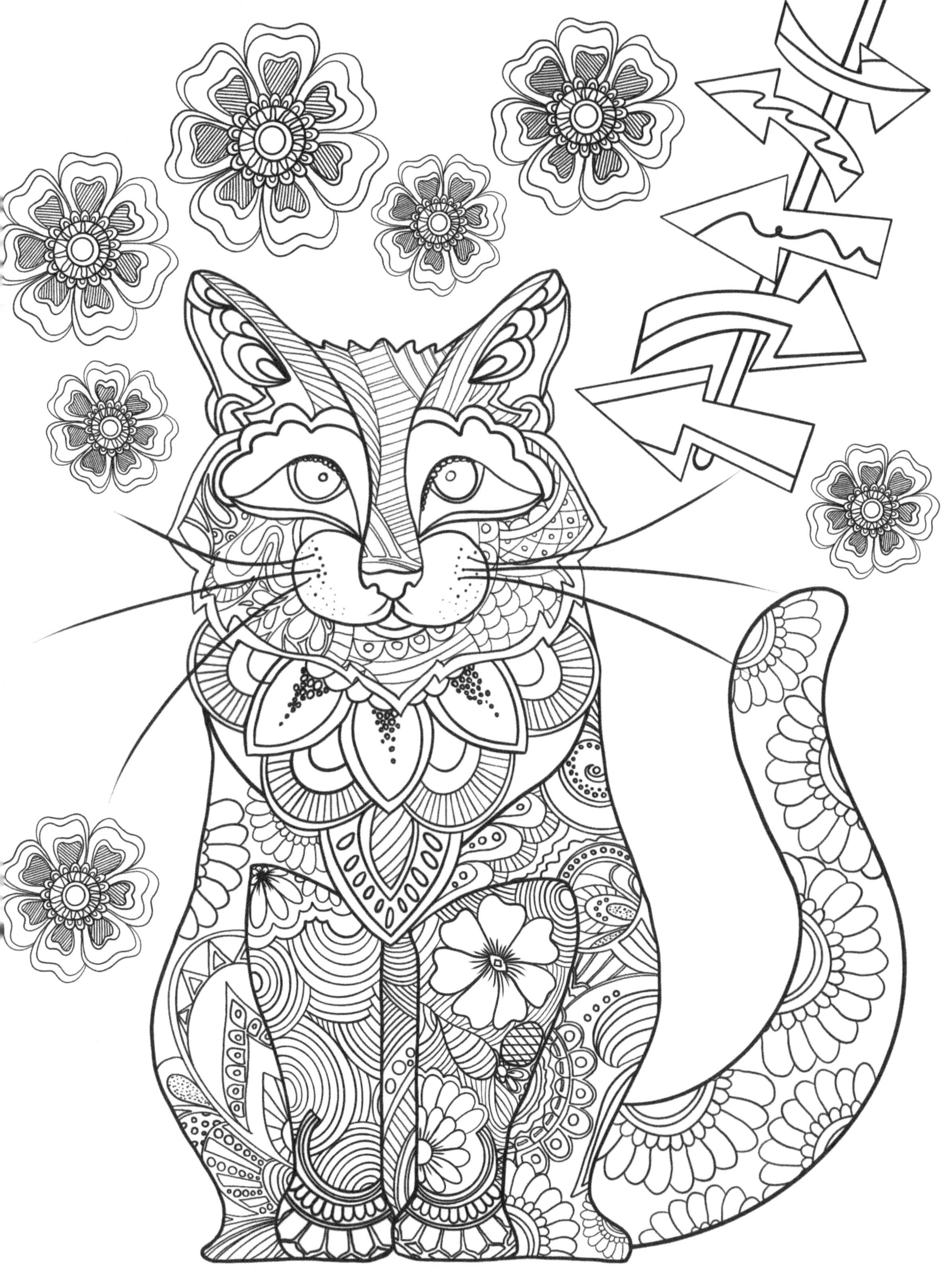

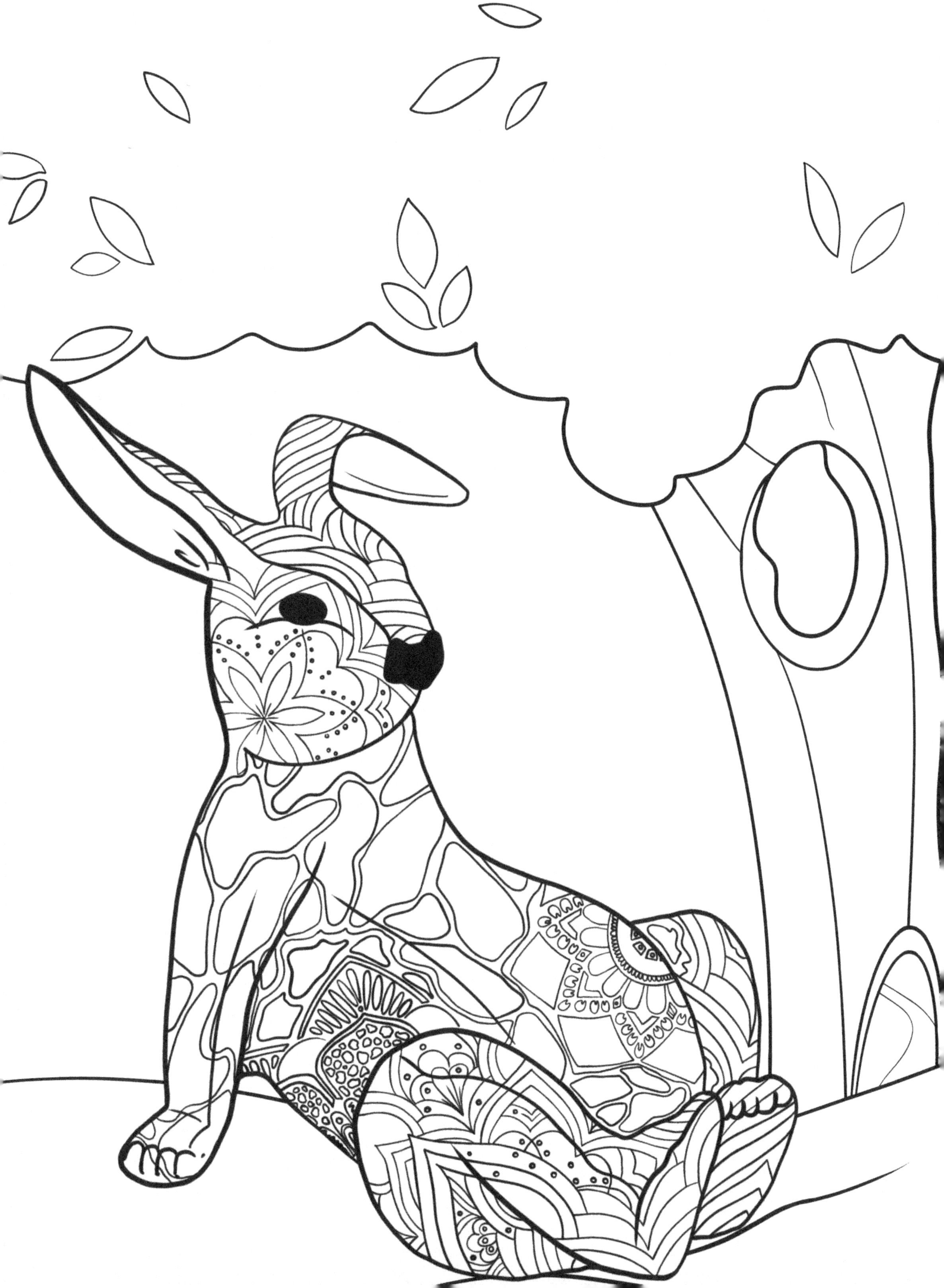

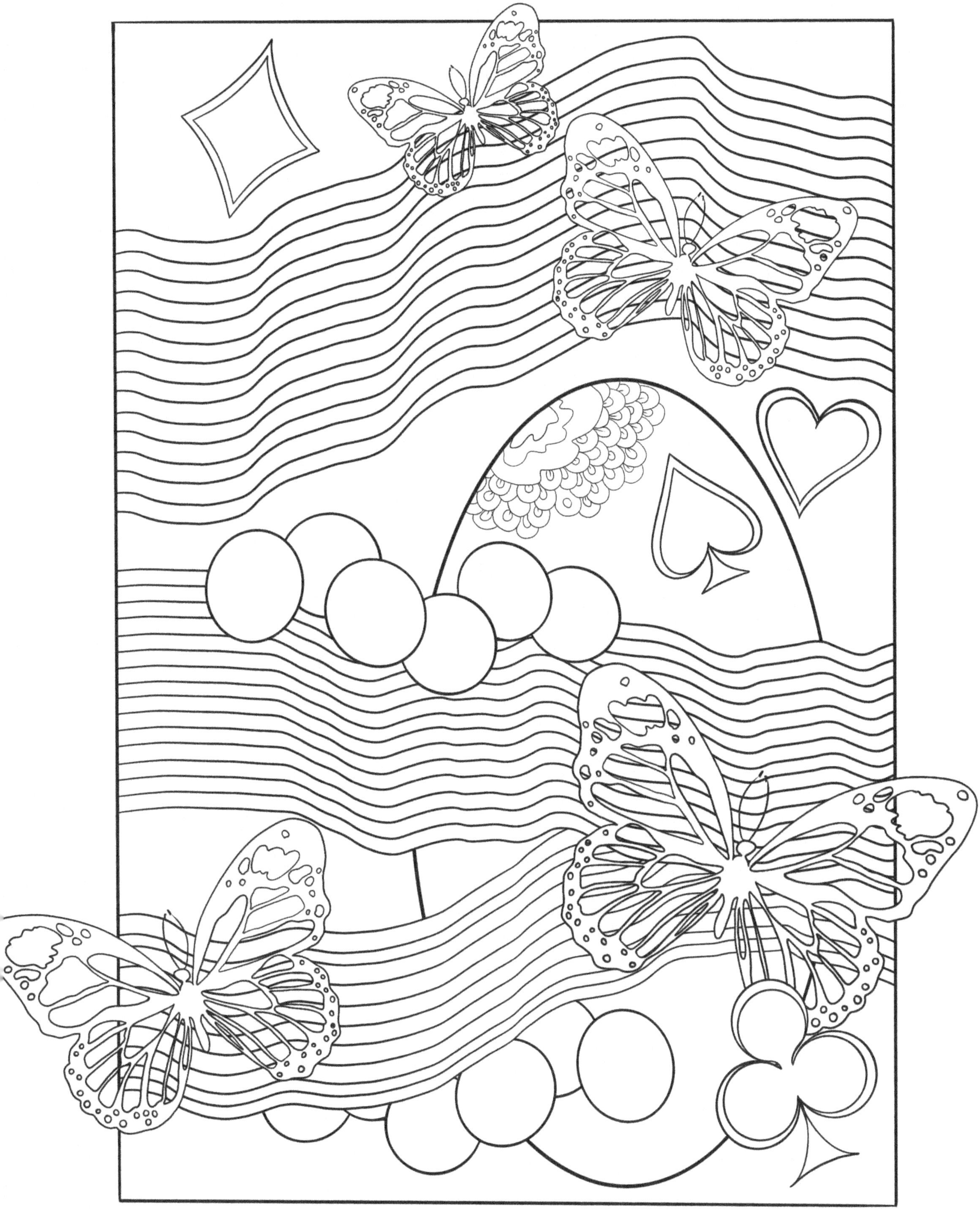

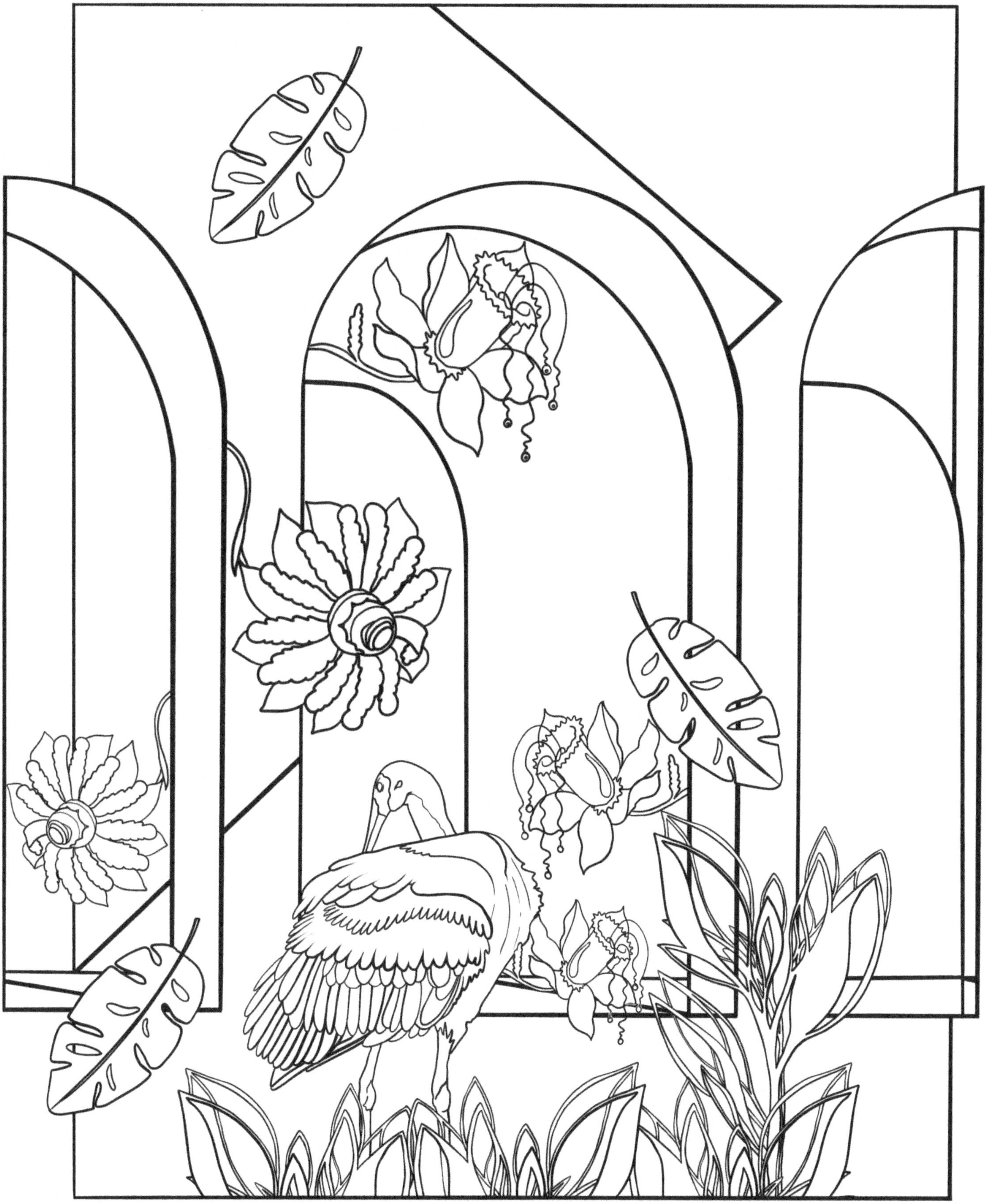

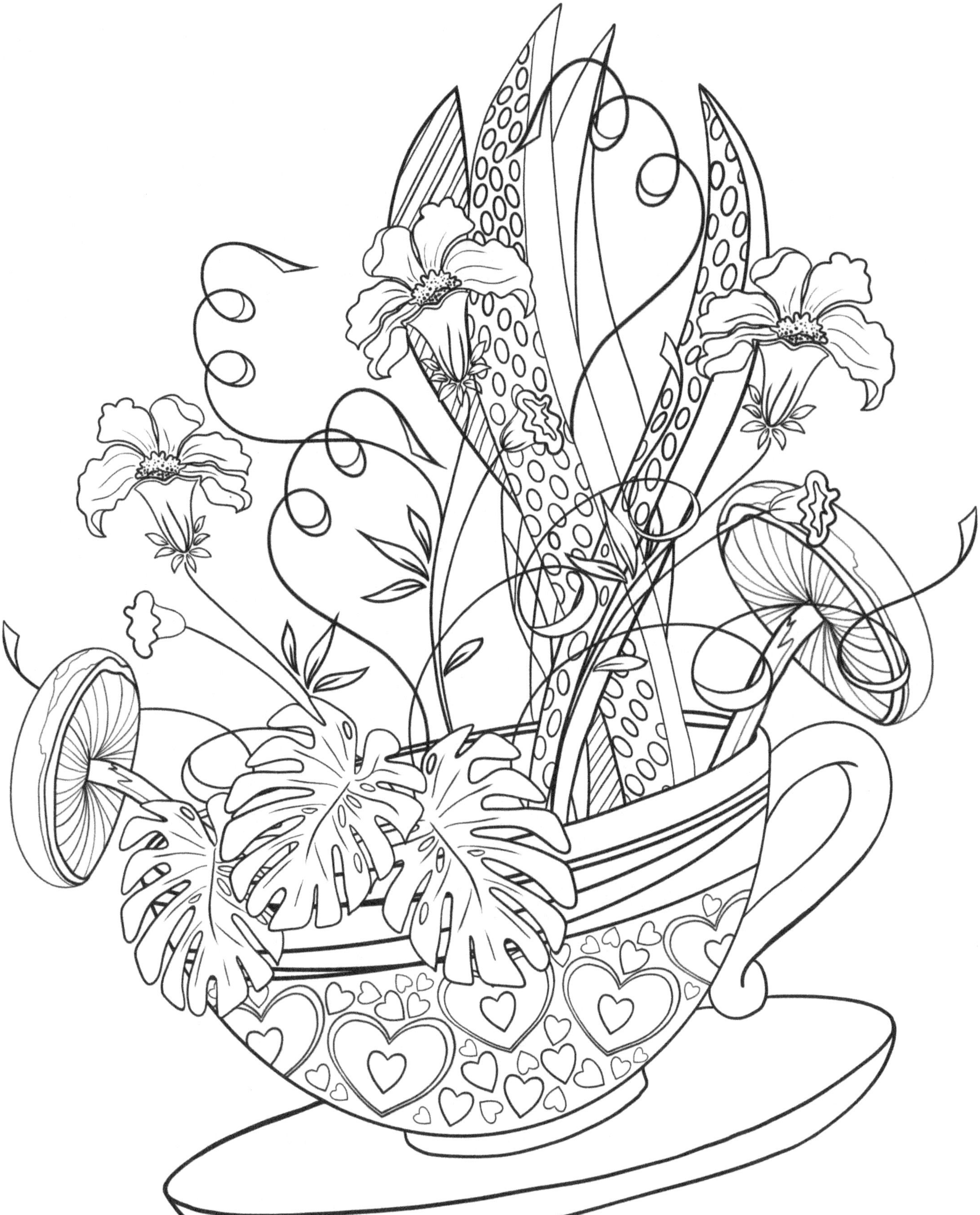

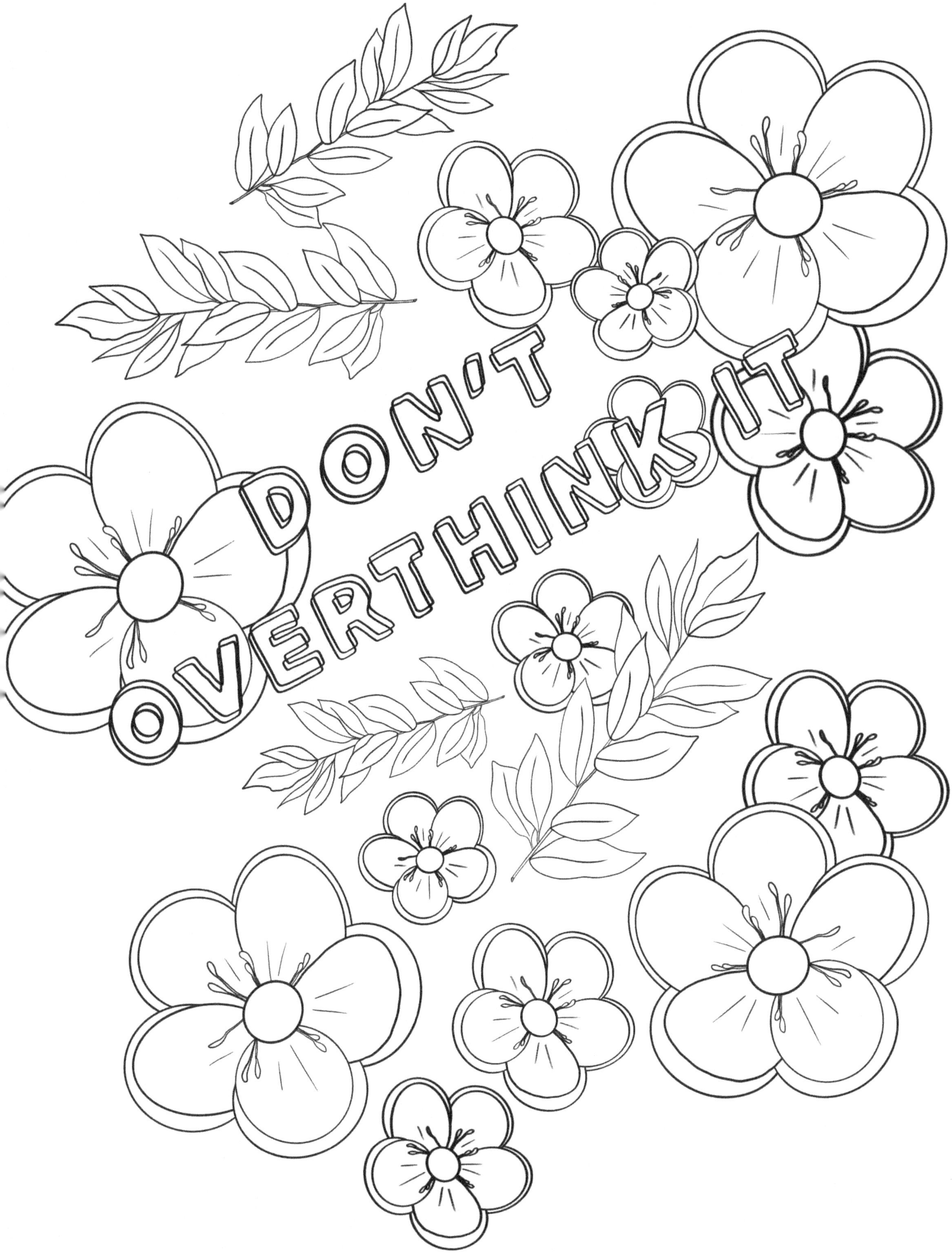
DON'T
OVERTHINK IT

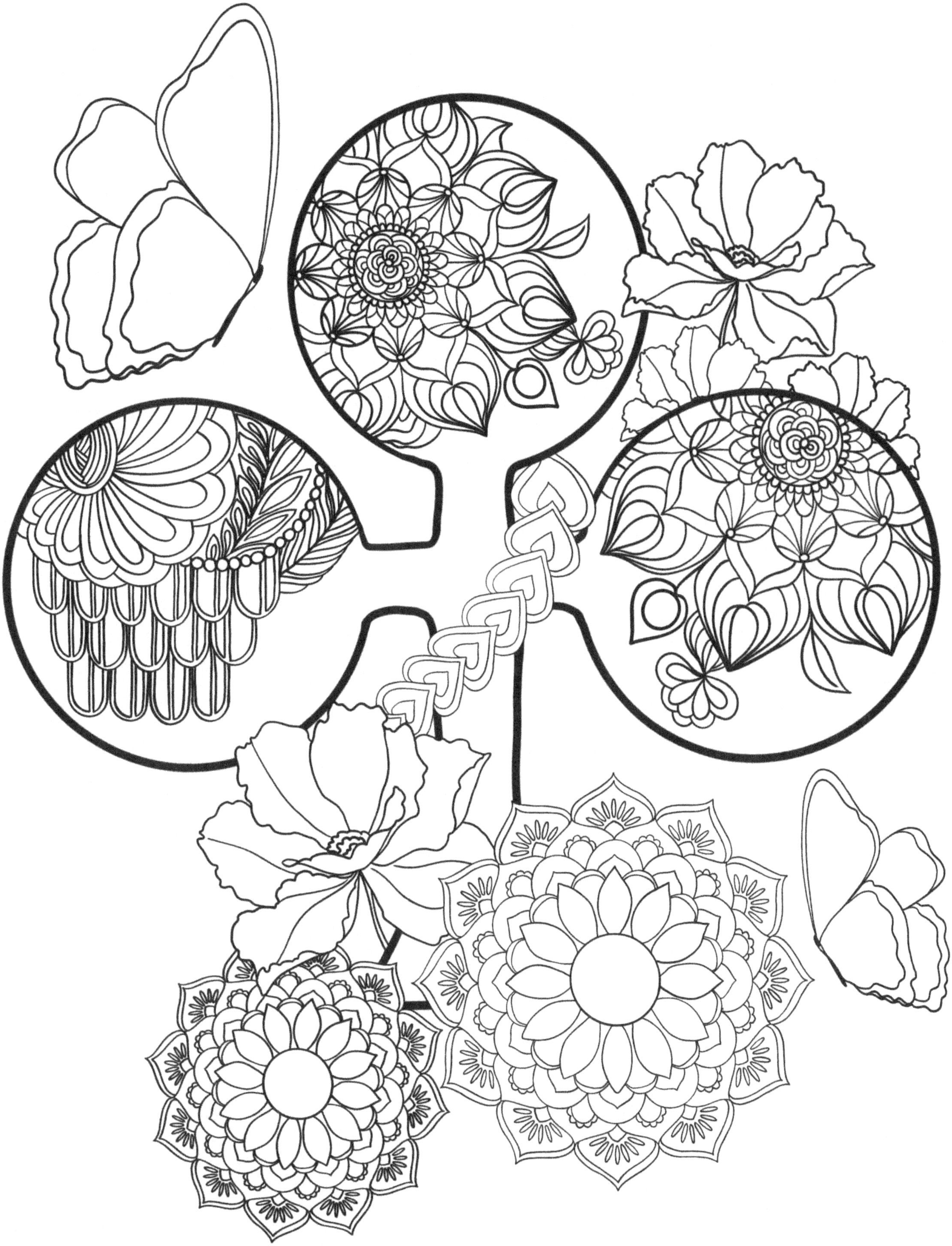

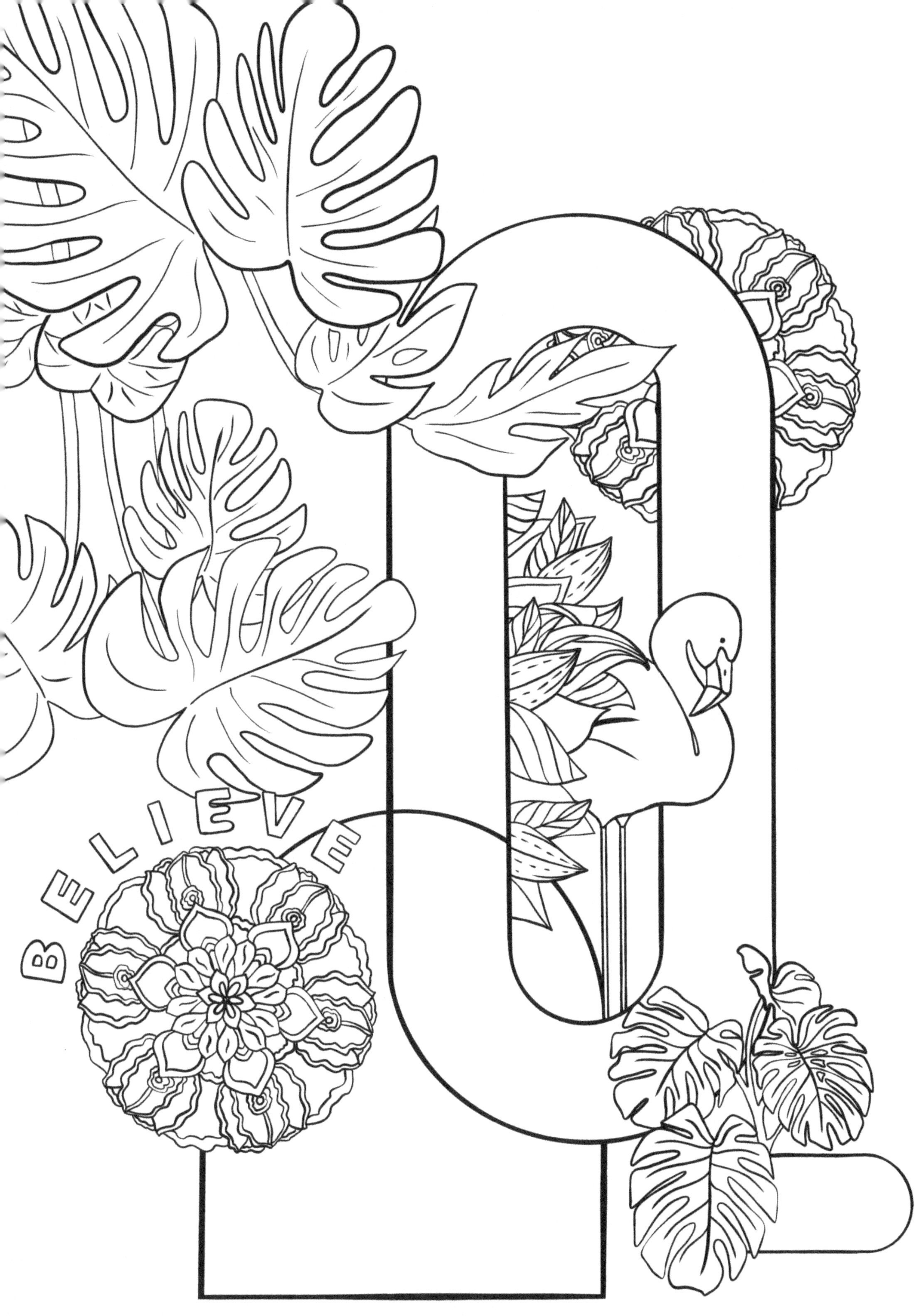
BELIEVE

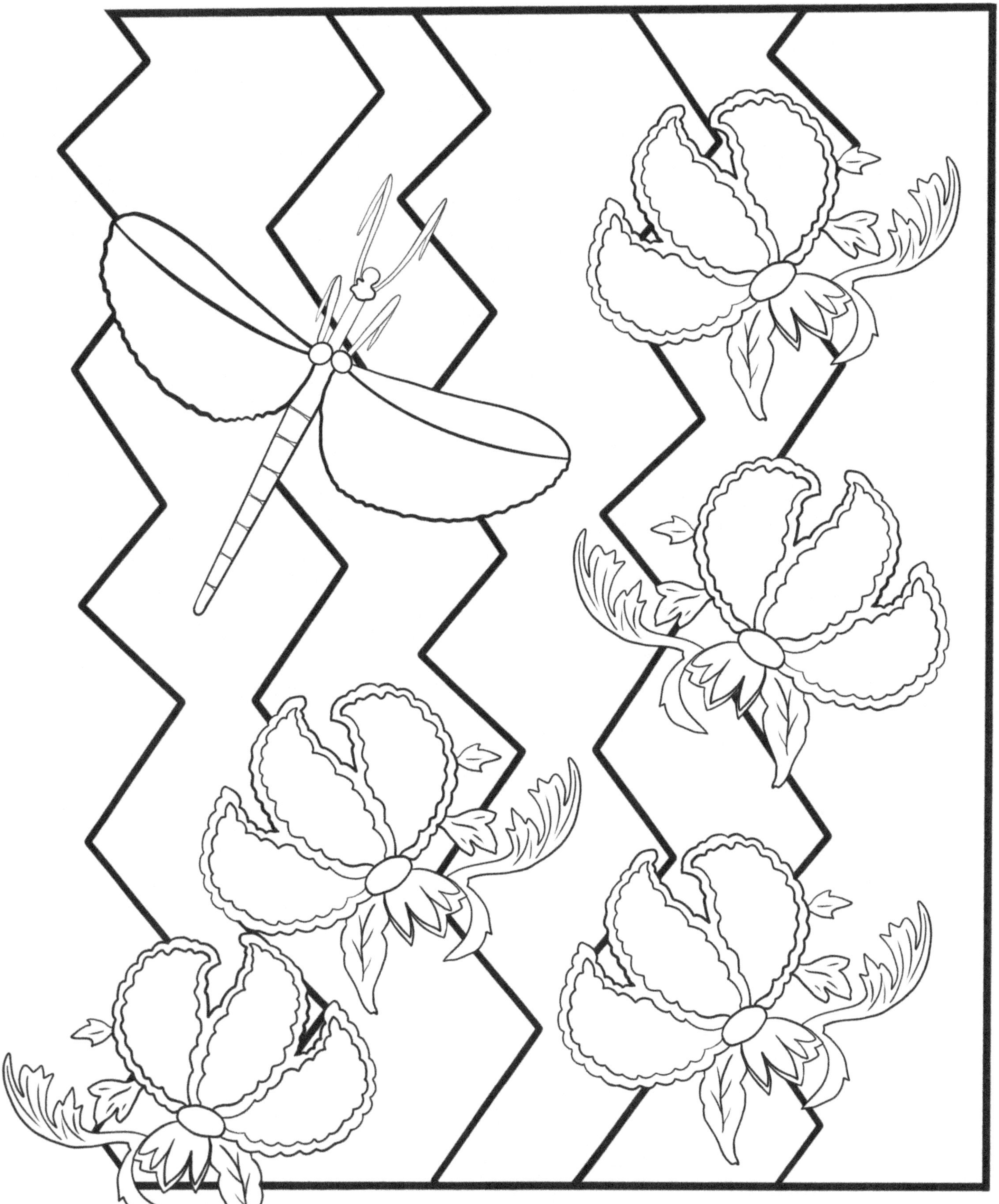

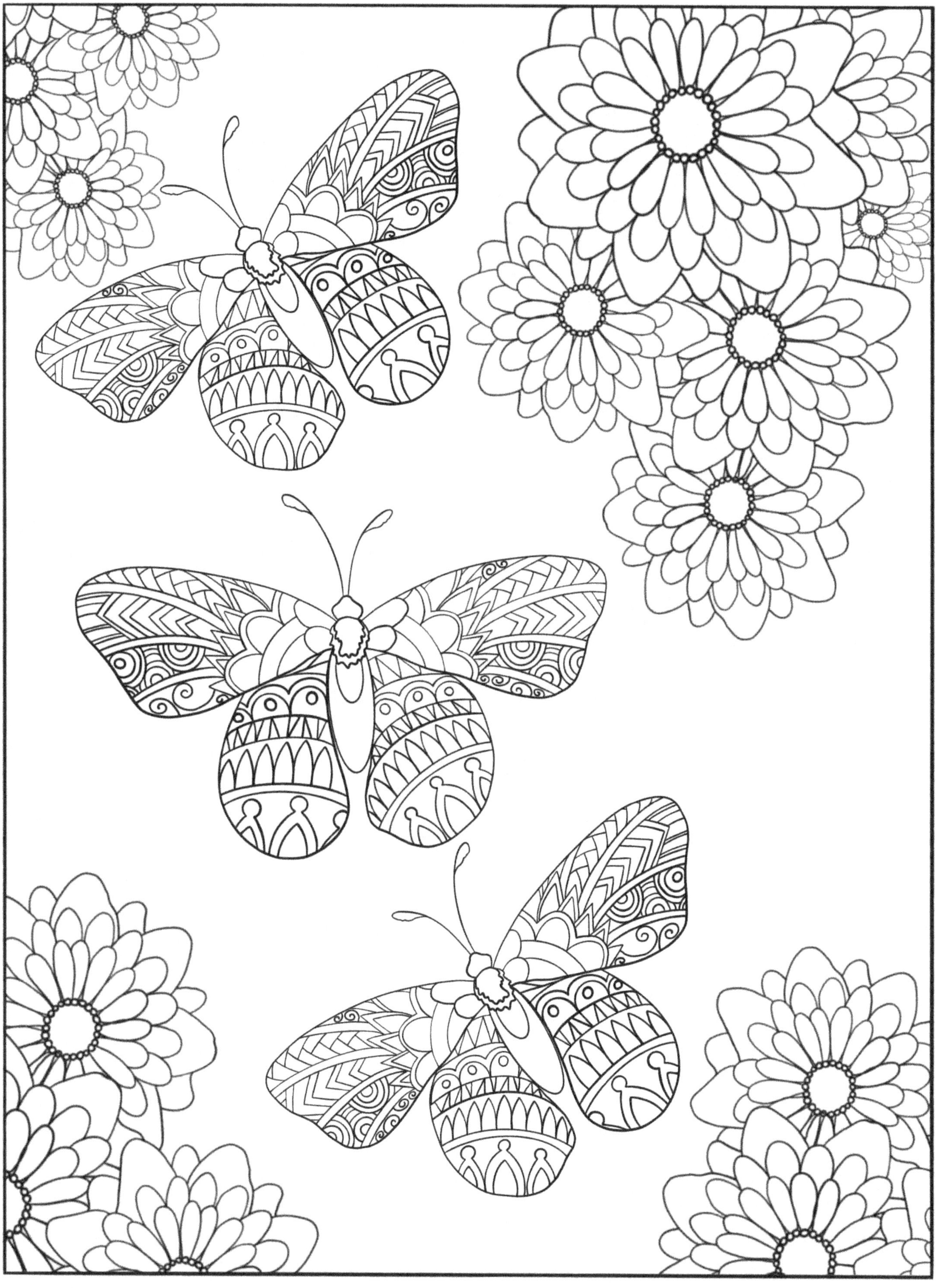

www.ingramcontent.com/pod-product-compliance
Lightning Source LLC
Chambersburg PA
CBHW081655220526
45466CB00009B/2766